COUNTRY BANKER

Country Banker

by

Mary Rattray

ARGYLL AND BUTE LIBRARY SERVICE

Published with the assistance of
Bank of Scotland

2001

First published in 2001 by Argyll and Bute Library Service
Library Headquarters
Highland Avenue
Sandbank
Dunoon
PA23 8PB

ISBN 1-903041-03-1

Argyll
Bute
COUNCIL

BANK OF SCOTLAND

Cover design courtesy of
the Ann Thomas Gallery, Tarbert, Argyll

Printed and bound by M. Downie & Son, Glasgow

Dedication

For Iain,
who can tell them better than I can.

With all my love,

MR

CONTENTS

Acknowledgements

Publication of this book would not have been possible without the generous financial assistance of Bank of Scotland and the enthusiasm of their archivist and publicity department.

I am indebted to Angus MacVicar for his encouragement and enthusiasm for my writing. Thanks also to Michael Davis (Argyll and Bute Library Service) for agreeing to publish the book in the first place, and to Eleanor Harris (Local Studies Librarian, Argyll and Bute Library Service) for editing the manuscript and bringing it to publication.

PREFACE

Throughout our marriage we have had young friends and relatives spending part of their holidays with us and Iain has kept them entertained by telling them stories of his early days in the bank. As they grew older they became aware that the advent of information technology meant that the world he spoke of was irretrievably lost, and they begged him to put his stories down on paper to preserve the record.

When he reached his eightieth birthday I realised that if this material was to be saved I was going to have to write it myself. I knew all the best stories of course, from much repetition, but I have had to quiz Iain unmercifully to obtain a proper understanding of the background. However, the result does have his approval now that he has corrected my mistakes and misunderstandings.

What cannot be retrieved is the tolerant humour, the gentle mimicry and the twinkle in the eye that make him such a compelling storyteller. Someone once said that Iain's secret is that he *likes* people: old and young, rich and poor, clever and limited. He enjoys them all. I hope that even a little of this has slipped past his stern censorship.

My husband was actually christened John. He adopted the Gaelic form of the name when he was called-up. However, as he has now been 'Iain' for over fifty years I thought it simpler to use this version throughout. Apologies are due to his relatives who still use his given name and to the diminishing number of pre-war friends who knew him as 'Jack' or 'Jacky'.

1

Oban – The Apprentice

'Will you take the boy into the business, Dave?' asked the Dunollie Road minister as they set up the chessmen for another game.

'No,' replied his friend, 'There's no future in tailoring.'

Although David Rattray had a thriving tailor's business in Oban, and employed eight or nine assistants in the height of the season, he had seen the writing on the wall when Burton's opened and for the first time it became possible to buy ready-made suits in the town. Now, in 1931, he saw the queues outside the employment exchange stretching down George Street, and growing longer by the day, and he worried what the future might hold for his young family.

He had already brought up one family, seen them safely launched and been widowed, before he moved up to take charge of the tailoring department in Chalmers, which was the store in Oban. Things had gone well for him, and he had married Maria McIver who had borne him a son and a daughter while he was in his fifties; but his heart was not in good shape, and he had been lying, 'at death's door', in one room while Maria was giving birth to Isobella in the other. Nevertheless, he had recovered – to open his own business and establish a reputation as a kiltmaker and ladies' tailor.

All the same, he was worried. He was now sixty-nine, and Iain was sixteen – and in all likelihood the boy would have to care for his mother and sister when his father's heart finally gave in. His son was good at figures and he would have liked to have seen him trained as a chartered accountant, but that would have meant supporting him in Glasgow for many years, and David wasn't at all sure that he had enough years left.

He talked to his cousin, who worked in the National Bank of Scotland somewhere in the Borders.

'Put the laddie in the bank, Dave,' was his advice.

Then word came that the Union Bank was about to open a branch in Oban. Of the eight banks operating in Scotland at that time, the Union was the only one not represented in the town. Yet it held the Argyll County Council account. In such a large and scattered county, the various council departments were divided between the larger towns. It would be far more convenient if the Union Bank had branches in all these centres. The council had been bringing pressure to bear for some time.

Now the decision had been taken. A new branch was to be opened in George Street Oban on 6th April 1931. The new Agent had already been appointed; he was to be Mr Robb, previously at Murrayfield, Edinburgh. Not altogether surprisingly, the accountant was to be the son of the County Clerk, who had served his apprenticeship in the Lochgilphead office, but there was a vacancy for a new apprentice.

David Rattray saw his chance and took it. On Saturday 4th April he sent Iain for a haircut and on the Sunday he said, casually. 'By the way, you'd better put on your good suit again in the morning. I've arranged an interview for you with Mr Robb.'

So, duly attired in his best blue serge suit (made by his father), a clean shirt with its stiff collar fastened back and front with studs and a sober tie, Iain presented himself at the newly-opened bank the next morning to find himself one of four applicants for the vacancy.

The examination was held on Monday 13th April, and consisted of papers in English, Mathematics and Geography, the latter of the 'capes and bays' variety. Iain was able to place all the names he was given on the maps provided, except Milford Haven and St Abb's Head, and he felt he had not done too badly. In this he was justified, as on the Thursday he was told that he had been successful and was sent to Dr Drysdale (known in Oban as 'the fouter') for a medical. After the most minimal examination the doctor gave him a penny and said, 'Away down to the weighing machine on the Esplanade, weigh yourself and come back with the ticket.'

He got the result at lunch-time on the following Tuesday, went to the shop to tell his father, and from there to the bank, where he was told to start the next day. At no time in this process was the boy himself consulted, nor was he unduly concerned about this. He couldn't stay at school forever and had no strong ideas of his own, so he went with the tide.

Mr Robb scrutinised him carefully when he arrived the next morning. He was neatly turned out – his father had seen to that, nothing to complain of there – so he was not particularly worried when the manager greeted him with, 'Right now, let me have a look at you. Good. Remember, no red ties, no brown shoes and – where's your hat?'

'I haven't got a hat, sir,' Iain stammered.

'Then you must go into Black and Skinner's at lunch-time and buy one, I don't expect to see you in the street bareheaded.'

How he hated that hat! Apart from the fact that it had cost half his first week's wages, it made him feel a 'right idiot'. As he hurried home along the main street he felt that everyone was looking at him, so he kept his head down to avoid recognition. He had got as far as Chalmers when he saw a crowd of boys from his class approaching, so he dashed up Argyll Street to avoid them.

If neatness in appearance was important, neatness in his work was vital. He was presented with two new pens with clean nibs. (He only realised later what a favour that was – clean nibs were like gold dust!) One pen was for ordinary ink and one for copying ink and to these were added a pencil and a rubber, but on no account was work done in ink to be erased. It had to be right first time. Then he was shown to his desk. All the desks in the main office were 'high' desks and it was usual to work standing up.

The process of copying a letter was complicated and took some skill. All letters leaving the bank were written by hand, either by the manager or the accountant, in copying ink. The letter-book was hard-backed but contained about 200 pages of tissue-like paper. A page was wetted with a brush and covered with blotting paper and a sheet of waterproof paper, on both sides, before being placed in the letter-press to extract the surplus water. When the page had acquired the requisite degree of dampness, the letter was inserted between the upper sheet of blotting paper and the page and the whole returned to the letter-press so that, if all went well, the damp paper picked up the imprint of the letter. If anything went wrong the poor apprentice had to approach his senior and ask him to re-write the whole thing. He was scared stiff the first time he tried it!

As all letters were hand-written, good clear handwriting was essential, and each apprentice was given a copy-book of the type used in schools and ordered to practice his handwriting whenever he had a moment to spare. Every month a sample of each apprentice's writing was sent up to Head Office for examination, until the officials there declared themselves satisfied that his handwriting would not disgrace the bank.

By the end of the day his head was reeling, and he was glad to escape until he had to run the gauntlet of his school chums, wearing his stiff collar and his new trilby hat.

The following day he was set the task of addressing the envelopes for the customers' passbooks.

'Now remember, you must not apply the term "Esquire" indiscriminately. Keep it for those to whom it clearly applies – the rest get "Mr".'

Iain interpreted these obscure instructions to confirm his impression that the world was divided into 'those, and such as those'; 'those' being the gentry, the highly paid professionals and the wealthier businessmen, and 'such as those' being the rest. This being so, he had no hesitation when he came to his father's name in addressing him as Mr David Rattray. David had, of course transferred his account when Iain was appointed: no doubt that was part of the deal!

Mr Robb was horrified. 'Good gracious boy! Have you no

respect for your own father. Tear that up at once! Your father *always* gets "Esquire", and don't you forget it!'

An essential skill, of course, was the ability to 'score' notes. Counting notes was done differently in Scottish banks, where the notes to be counted were held firmly in the left hand, clear of the desk, and counted off in twenties at great speed with the right. These, folded in half and showing the back of the outside note, were secured with an elastic band – hence the term 'scoring'. If a lesser number was left, they were secured with the top note top-side out to indicate that the score was incomplete.

Many years later Norval Charteris, who was the manager at Campbeltown, told a story of his appearance as a bank clerk in a play that was competing at a drama festival. The adjudicator was very critical of his performance and told him, 'At the very least, you should go into a bank and get them to show you the *right* way to count notes. That was totally unconvincing.' The adjudicator was an Englishman, and the English way was to hold the notes firmly on the counter with one hand and count the upper right corners with the other. Nowadays, the notes are just put through a machine and the counting is done automatically.

There was ample opportunity to compete in this skill at the daily 'exchange and clearing' which was held in a room hired by the banks for the purpose. For many years the Oban clearing was held in a room above Boots the Chemists. This process was also peculiar to Scottish banks. Because there were eight banks, all issuing their own notes, it was inevitable that at the end of the day each bank would be holding a fair number of notes belonging to competing banks. By law, each bank could issue only its own notes and Bank of England one pound and ten-shilling notes, and each bank had to pay a nominal stamp duty for each note in circulation, that is, not in its own possession. Therefore, it was in the interest of all the banks to get their own notes back as fast as they could.

The local clearing house was fitted with eight desks, one for each bank, and each morning, from Tuesday to Saturday, two clerks from each bank met to exchange notes. It gave Iain the opportunity to meet the other apprentices and he was delighted when Willie Ford joined the Bank of Scotland and Charlie Carmichael the Commercial Bank. He was not now the only one of his age group condemned to wear a hat; indeed Charlie was worse off as he had to wear a bowler.

On Saturdays there was a 'second exchange' at the close of business, so that each bank had the maximum number of its own notes in hand when it sent up its weekly return to Head Office. It was on the basis of these returns that the bank was charged for notes in circulation by the Treasury.

The morning all the exchange clerks feared most was the day after a staff member of the Clydesdale Bank on Mull came over to the mainland on holiday as he brought with him all the notes that had been amassed on the island since his last visit, and the exchange on that day took ages.

It was not only notes that were transported from bank to bank. In those days, a pound was a lot of money and most everyday transactions involved the use of coin. The thing about coin was that it was *heavy*. Supplies from Head Office had to be transported by rail, and the charges were exorbitant. Therefore, it was only in the most desperate of circumstances that extra coin was obtained from that source. Normally it would be 'bought' (with notes) from another bank that was carrying a surplus. The Union Bank had the accounts of several multiples such as Cooper's, R S McColl and the Buttercup Dairy, and, during the summer months, these required very large quantities of change.

A not infrequent sight therefore, in the busy summer months, was that of the bank apprentice dressed in his good suit and, of course, his hat, pushing a large wooden garden wheelbarrow, with a noisy iron wheel, up the main street of Oban. Piled on the barrow were sacks of coin, and trailing behind there would be an escort of jeering wee boys!

This was not such a security hazard as might at first appear. In the first place, coin, as has been pointed out, is heavy and a potential thief could not run very fast carrying a sack of silver or copper. Get-away cars were the stuff of movies. The number of cars in Oban could still be counted and were known, and a strange one would have aroused intense interest. In any case, there were only two roads out of the town, one north and one south, and neither was exactly a motorway. The thieves would be lucky if they travelled ten miles before they were caught, assuming they were outsiders. Insiders would be recognised by everyone in the street.

Nevertheless, it was fascinating being in at the beginning of a new branch, and the aforementioned stores were already customers of the Union Bank before the Oban branch was opened and so provided, together with the County Council and its many employees, a solid foundation on which to build. After that, it was up to the manager to build up the business by personal contact, and Mr Robb's social life was hectic, as was the accountant's. Even Iain was pressured into donning a dinner jacket to count the takings at a whist-drive held by the ladies of 'The Eastern Star' [female relatives' order of the Masons], when the manager found himself double-booked. Also, callous as it may seem, even funerals provided a frequent opportunity for contact with customers – and prospective customers. On these occasions Mr Robb appeared in the office wearing a tile hat and a frock coat, but then, so did Iain's father. Moreover, he kept a frock coat in the shop and wore it when he was dealing with important customers. They were formal times!

As his parents had retired to Mull, the agent went over there almost every week-end to visit them and to drum up custom. Iain became used to the instruction, 'Nip down to the pier, boy, and ask Mr Black to delay sailing for a few minutes. I'm coming as fast as I can.' Mr Black was the purser of *Lochinvar*, the steamer that made the daily run to Mull.

David MacBrayne (1928) Ltd was another of the bank's main customers and many of the tradesmen who had worked on the alterations to the building before the branch opened were also prevailed upon to open accounts. So, at the end of the first year, the bank's inspectors were well enough pleased with the progress that had been made, but were looking for more. The population of Argyll was so scattered, however, that once all the prospective customers in the town had been accounted for, further growth could come only from the outlying areas. The few roads were bad, and most public transport, apart from the railway, depended on the ferries.

Some of the established banks had sub-offices, which were invariably on the railway line, so that clerks could travel easily between the main branch and its subsidiary. The British Linen Bank had a sub-office at Benderloch, while the Commercial Bank had sub-offices at Taynuilt, Loch Awe and Dalmally.

Mr Robb had the use of his father's *Vulcan* car, and he had visionary ideas. He took the inspectors to Easdale and Kilmelford. Both these sizeable villages lay on the road south from Oban and were not served by the railway. 'But,' he argued, 'they could be reached by a van which served as a mobile bank. That way only two members of staff would be needed to perform the function of a sub-office in both communities – and we could steal a march on the other banks, who are tied to the railway.'

The inspectors laughed him to scorn: surely he couldn't be serious? 'It would be like turning the bank into a fish and chip shop,' they said. Much later, bank vans were to become a well recognised feature of Highland banking. Mr Robb was ahead of his time.

Life was not all work. Iain and his great friend Jimmy Black, who had found work in the office of the Oban Times just down the lane from the bank, spent their summer evenings on the golf course and winter evenings at the pictures or rehearsing with the Oban Old Parish Church Dramatic and Comedy Society.

As far as the banks were concerned, the great social event of the year was the Bankers' Dance. This was organised by the accountants of the eight banks and held in the Royal Hotel each January. It was patronised by all the lawyers and the leading businessmen of the town and was extremely formal. The apprentices were all there in their dinner jackets – but not to dance! It was their job to take the tickets at the door and man the cloakrooms and the bar.

Even so, Iain was met at the door by Mr Robb and his appearance inspected. 'Just a minute! Let me have a look at you. Tie tied properly? Turn round – let me look at your shoes. Right, you'll do.' All this before he was allowed to progress into the hotel. He was lucky. His father had made his suit and provided the necessary boiled shirt and gold studs and cuff-links, but it must have been hard for apprentices on £40 per year to meet the required standard. They wouldn't have dared to ask any of the assembled ladies to dance. They were there to make themselves useful as unobtrusively as possible! It is perhaps not surprising that Iain came to hate formal entertaining and 'dressing-up'.

Dressing-up for dramatic purposes was a different matter, but even then, the more disreputable his costume, the happier he was. He became increasingly involved with 'the drama', the shorthand version of the club's more ambitious title. This became a problem when it conflicted with the bank exams.

The trouble was that the dramatic clubs put on their shows in the middle of winter and the bank's exams were in March. There was a degree of competition between the two, especially in his final year. Having taken a part in the Christmas Show, *Rob Roy*, he was prevailed upon to take a minor part in the one-act play, *Dr Abernethie*, for the local Scottish Community Drama Association's competitive festival in February. Unfortunately, his team won the festival and had to go on to the Divisional Final in Glasgow the following month. It was uncomfortably near to his final bank examination. Fortunately, though his team was unsuccessful, he did pass the examination, though there was some anxious nail-biting before the results came out on the first of May.

By means of some sadistic genius, the Bank Examination results arrived in the offices on the day the banks were closed for the Scottish May Bank Holiday and so were inaccessible to juniors, who carried no keys. The accountant, or the manager had to be coaxed to go down to the bank and open up to collect the mail, before the verdict could be known.

Yet the examinations had their advantages. All the apprentices in the town travelled together to Glasgow the night before the exams, and great were the celebrations once they were safely over. In Iain's third year, some of the boys proposed that they should sit their examinations in Edinburgh and take the opportunity to see something of the capital. I don't think that any of them had been there before.

The examination was held in a hall in George Heriot's School and it was excessively formal. It was invigilated by retired bank men in black jackets and striped trousers, one of whom read out the rules in a voice of doom at the outset ending with, 'If you have a need to visit the gentlemen's room, you will stand in your place and point to the door marked "Gentlemen" and wait to be escorted.'

An hour or so into the examination, the only young lady in a roomful of several hundred students stood meekly and pointed to the door of the 'Ladies'. The looks of horror on the faces of the invigilators caused the whole room to erupt in gales of laughter. It was a long time before girl apprentices became commonplace.

2
Tarbert and Killin

As Iain drew nearer to the end of his apprenticeship, he became available to do 'relief' at other branches, experience of differing kinds of business being regarded as an essential part of a boy's training. Thus when he was sent to Tarbert for two months in the summer of 1935, he expected to find that the business would be different; what he didn't expect was that the whole atmosphere of the office would be happier but, to his delight, it was!

First he had to get there. The straightforward way would be to get the bus to Lochgilphead and another to Tarbert, but there was a snag. The Saturday before the Monday he was due to start was the day of the quarterly balance. This meant that he would be working until six o'clock, at least; too late for the last bus to Lochgilphead. There were no buses to Lochgilphead on a Sunday, so he would have to make a round-about journey via Arrochar, and that would take all day. Tarbert is about fifty-five miles from Oban by the direct route! The bank paid his fare, but he had to travel in his own time.

'Digs' had been arranged for him with Mrs Cullen at *Wyndham*, a semi-detached villa on the Campbeltown Road. Mrs Cullen was looking out for him and took him straight to his room. 'It's been a long day for you, but come down as soon as you can. Your supper's ready and you'll feel better when you've had something to eat,' she said, kindly.

As he tucked in to his meal, he considered what he already

knew about his new branch, which wasn't much. It was a two-man office, catering for a fishing community and he was to stand in for the accountant, who was on holiday.

After some chat, he ventured to ask his landlady if she knew the agent, Mr Couper.

'Mr Couper?' she said, 'You'll get on fine with him, don't worry. It was a shame about his wife, though.'

'What happened?' he asked.

'She died when their little girl was born. That must be nearly five years ago; she'll be starting school after the holidays.'

'Who looks after them?' he asked, moved by this sad story.

'Oh, he has a good housekeeper, but it's not the same. Still he keeps busy, and he gets on well with the fishermen. So does Mr Cormack, come to that. He comes from Orkney and there's plenty of fishing there.'

Iain began to wonder how he would do. There were fishing boats at Oban, but fishing came well after tourism and agriculture in the scheme of things. Somehow he couldn't quite picture Mr Robb or Mr Sinclair hob-nobbing with the tough-looking men on the fish quay. He began to suspect that things might be different in Tarbert.

The next day he became certain of it. The atmosphere in the office was more relaxed altogether, and yet he sensed that Mr Couper was held in great respect by all the customers; and though his manner was warm and kindly, Iain wouldn't have been tempted to take any liberties.

Overall, this was a more efficient office than Oban. So he was surprised when, soon after the door was shut at three o'clock and the immediate tidying-up had been done, Mr Cooper said, 'Right, that'll do. Come on, I'll take you for a walk down to the pier. We can finish up after tea. I don't suppose you've fixed up anything special to do?'

Iain had brought his golf clubs, but he had still to locate the golf course and there was no hurry for that. He picked up his hat.

'Put that down, you won't need it while you're here,' said this astonishing man, and Iain needed no second bidding.

Mr Couper walked with a limp but he moved briskly enough in spite of it. As they walked along the harbour wall, he showed him the boatyard, flourishing in the hands of the Dickie brothers, and pointed out the shops owned by customers at the branch. Everyone seemed to know him and he had a word for them all. He was completely at home on the fish quay and, as they picked their way between the ropes and the nets, he greeted all the men on the quay by name, whether they were boat-owners or skippers or crew.

It soon became apparent that Mr Couper's social life was every bit as active as Mr Robb's, but different. Compared with Tarbert, Oban seemed to be a socially stratified community, and Mr Robb's activities were confined to the upper strata. No such gradations seemed to operate in Tarbert, where everyone knew everyone else and everything revolved around the fishing. Mr Couper mixed with everyone, from the poorest to the richest, though those terms seemed irrelevant in a village where everyone was related to everyone else.

As the days went on his admiration for his new manager

increased. He had been in awe of Mr Robb, but Mr Couper came to represent an ideal. The agent had worked in the law department of Head Office earlier in his career, and in this isolated village that had no lawyer and no chartered accountant in residence, he was frequently turned to for advice on matters not strictly within his province as a banker.

Iain came to realise this the day he was called in to witness a will being made by a blind man. Mr Couper had drawn up the will and had arranged for the minister to be present. When they were all assembled, the minister read the will aloud to the blind man and asked if it was in accordance with his wishes, and when he agreed that it was, the minister signed it. Mr Couper and Iain then signed that this had been done. Iain thought it must be wonderful to have the knowledge to be able to help people like that, and it added a new impetus to his studies in Scots law.

After his first four weeks in Tarbert, Mr Couper went on holiday and Mr Cormack, a tall, red-headed Orcadian, took charge of the branch. Iain was a bit wary of him at first. Even though he was only the accountant – he was old. He looked even older than Mr Couper. He was all of thirty-six! He was a keen golfer, however, and ready to give the boy a game. Preparation was being made and teams were being picked for the annual matches with Tighnabruaich, a matter that needed some diplomacy. It wasn't just a matter of choosing the best players. Care had to be taken to make sure that no-one on the team was teetotal. The teams travelled in a fishing boat and the celebrations after the match were every bit as important as the match itself. Each team visited the other once a year and similar reciprocal visits were made by the Masonic Lodges.

Iain spent his 21st birthday in Tarbert, and celebrated with a visit to the pictures, but he did get a Greetings telegram from home. It was the first that he had ever seen!

He must have looked young for his age, however. One lunch-time, when he was alone in the office, a lady from the Island of Gigha came in and looked him up and down in some disdain.

'Where's Mr Couper?' she demanded.

'He's on holiday,' Iain replied.

'Where's Mr Cormack?'

'He's just gone for his lunch,' he told her.

'Then who are you?'

'My name's Rattray, and I'm here from Oban to stand in for Mr Cormack.'

She took a moment to digest this information, then she asked suspiciously, 'Do you know Mr Lindsay?'

Mr Lindsay was the headmaster of Tarbert School, but Iain was able to reply, 'Oh, yes. He taught me science at Oban High School.'

That seemed to do the trick, for she said reluctantly, 'Then I suppose it will be all right,' – and paid five pounds into her account!

Just before he left, Mrs Cullen's other lodger, the domestic science teacher at the school, returned to start the new term. She was pleasant and friendly, and some time later Iain was delighted to learn that she had become the second Mrs Couper.

Life in Oban seemed even more stuffy after this experience and he longed for another opportunity to get away. This came in the middle of the winter, when he was sent on relief to Killin in Perthshire, far from the mitigating effects of the Gulf Stream on the Scottish climate.

It was bitterly cold and snowing hard as he neared his destination, but at least he had been able to make the journey by train, as at that time the main line from Oban to Glasgow passed through Killin Junction. From there, a single coach pulled by a small tank-engine took him down to Killin village, and a short tramp through the snow brought him to the boarding-house where he was to stay. When he went up to his bedroom that first night, ice coated the inside of the window-panes and the only source of heat was the stone hot water bottle, known as a 'pig', provided by his landlady. It was a relief to go down to breakfast next morning and find the room heated by a large anthracite stove and enjoy a fine hot breakfast served by a kindly cook/waitress who asked all the guests, 'Now, what would you like me to make for your meal tonight?' There were two other lodgers – a young man who worked in the Breadalbane Estate office and a lady of uncertain age who was manageress of the Mill Shop.

Like Tarbert, Killin was a two-man office with an adjoining bank house, and Iain was to provide holiday relief first for the accountant, and then the manager. The town consisted of one long street and served as an agricultural centre. It had an auction mart and two woollen mills, both powered by huge water-wheels driven by the fiercely running river that made the Falls of Dochart such an attractive feature to tourists in the summer. Thus the same river that drove the mills attracted fishermen to the hotels, and brought customers to the village to buy the product.

In those days when travel was more difficult than it is now, the railway was important to Killin. There was no bank (other than the weekly sub-offices) between Killin and Oban and farmers and hotel-keepers as far west as Tyndrum did their banking in Killin. The older schoolchildren travelled daily by train to school in Callander, and some people living between Killin and Callander chose to keep their accounts in the branch. In addition, it drew people who travelled by car or by trap from the lower reaches of Loch Tayside. All-in-all, it was a lively centre, but Iain missed the sea, as, apart from summer holidays with his aunt and uncle in Stirling, he had never lived inland before, and he felt hemmed-in.

He soon discovered that it was not only his digs that had no electricity. The whole town was wired up and the switches were in place on the wall ready for when the Grampian hydro-electric scheme came into operation, but for the moment they served a purely decorative function. Meanwhile, the office was heated by a large open fire, and the maid brought in an Aladdin lamp when the light started to fade.

Mr Lamont, the manager, was pleased to see him, but Iain was a bit surprised when he said, 'Just a minute – I'll need to introduce you to the dog.' He whistled, and a large, red setter bounded in from the house. 'This is Mr Rattray, he's a *friend*,' he said, and the dog obediently offered a paw. Iain took it and patted the dog, but it was the next morning before he realised the purpose of this strange introduction. As soon as he entered the office, the dog came in carrying a little leather pouch containing the bank's keys and laid them at his feet. The key turned the strong-room lock, but before the door would open Mr Lamont had to operate a huge screw in the floor of his bedroom, which screwed into the top corner of the strong-room door.

The telephone sat out in the hall and was shared by the bank house. It was connected to the exchange in the sub-post-office down the street. About to make a call, Iain asked the banker for the number, only to be told, 'Don't bother with a number – just lift the phone and tell Arthur to put you through.' Life in Oban was never like this!

There were two banks in Killin: the other was a slightly bigger office of the Bank of Scotland with a staff of two men and an apprentice. It was great weather for curling and both bank managers were curling fanatics and cheerfully went off curling during banking hours. If challenged they would have argued that you had to make use of the ice while you had it, and anyway it was an opportunity to meet the bank's customers. 'Meeting the bank's customers' gave a rural manager a lot of scope. This may have been because the banks were just changing from 'lawyer-agents' who were lawyers first and ran the bank as a side line, to managers who were full-time employees of the bank. For a long time the new men continued to be called 'the Agent' and to act as if they still had the freedom of the self-employed.

As he went off first thing next morning, leaving Iain to man the office single-handed, Mr Lamont gave him basic instructions, adding, 'If you need someone to go a message, phone the Bank of Scotland and their boy will come over, and my wife will watch the place while you have your lunch.'

As it had been impressed upon him, time and time again, that all bank business must be kept confidential even from one's nearest and dearest, perhaps *especially* from one's nearest and dearest, Iain was flabbergasted. However, on the dot of twelve o'clock, in came Mrs Lamont. She begged a cigarette, settled down with her knitting, and said, 'Don't worry, if anyone comes in I'll tell them you'll be back in twenty minutes. They all know where he is anyway.'

Iain wondered what their respective Head Offices would say if they were aware of this degree of fraternisation. Helping each other out with change was one thing, but sharing staff was quite another. He hoped fervently that they would not get caught, but they very nearly did. One morning, about a quarter to ten, the inspector walked in. Iain felt quite sick when he realised who it was but the agent took it in his stride.

The possibility that the inspector would be on the morning train had been borne in mind when the arrangements were made for the curlers to meet at ten o'clock as by that time they could be sure he was not coming that day. Mrs Lamont could be relied upon to get a message to the other bank, but it put paid to the curling for the next two days.

Nevertheless, Mr Lamont had his serious side. It was he who suggested that Iain should sit for the English qualification. 'You're going to find time heavy on your hands in the winter now they've started moving you about. Why don't you use it to get your English Member's? You're exempt from a lot of it now you've passed your Scottish finals. It won't do you any harm if you are looking for promotion.' Neither Mr Robb nor Mr Sinclair held this qualification, but an earlier accountant at Killin had taken the examination, so Mr Lamont knew all about it. Iain took his advice and sent away for the correspondence lessons.

Mr Robb gave him another unexpected piece of advice. Apropos of nothing at all, he said one day, 'You'll have noticed that my wife and I get along very well?' Surprised, Iain said that he had indeed noticed this. 'That's because our nearest relatives live in Greenock. If you ever get married, take my advice and never live within a hundred miles of your nearest relatives.'

Marriage couldn't have been farther from his thoughts, but the younger man agreed that he would bear it in mind. In fact, he couldn't have got married even if he had wanted to. No clerk could marry without permission from Head Office. This was not given before a man's salary reached £200, at age 27 or 28, and then only on condition that he moved to one of the larger Scottish cities, Glasgow, Edinburgh, Dundee, Aberdeen or Perth. This meant that he could be moved from one branch to another without the expense of moving house.

Iain had heard a sad story of a clerk in the Commercial Bank whose mother had died and whose father had offered to make up his salary so that he could marry his fiancée and she could move in and look after them both. The young lady was quite agreeable to this arrangement, but the bank refused permission. Not surprisingly he left the service.

One evening the lad in the digs asked him if he would like to go to the pictures that night.

'I didn't know you had a cinema,' Iain said.

'We do once a week. The travelling cinema comes to the village hall,' he replied, and Iain agreed that it sounded fun.

When they left their digs they joined a crowd of people making their way up the street, most of them carrying cushions under their arms. Once inside, he soon realised why, as the wooden benches which provided the only seating were pretty hard. The power needed to show the film was provided by an old lorry that was parked just outside the building, and he soon learned to arrive early enough to obtain a seat on the far side of the hall since, if one's seat was too close to the lorry, the dialogue was drowned out by the noise of the engine. But it was a cheerful social occasion and what it lacked in sophistication, it made up for in good company.

It was getting near to Christmas and his time in Killin was drawing to a close. Before he left, the kindly manageress of the woollen mill shop, with whom he had shared so many hot breakfasts, helped him to choose presents for the family at far below the prices he would have paid for them in Chalmers in Oban.

He had travelled home on the train the previous week-end and his father had lent him the car to return to Killin, so that he could get away immediately after work, but the journey down from Oban had been horrendous, as the snow got worse the nearer he got to Killin. The only vehicle that had travelled ahead of him was an Alexander's bus, and its tracks were too wide to be of help to a

1926 *Baby Austin*. The small car had made heavy work of forcing its way through the snow and, having no windscreen wipers, he had been forced to get out to clear the windscreen with increasing frequency. There was no heater in the car and the collapsible hood was far from being windproof, so at one point he had been forced to get out and run up and down for ten minutes in the snow to get some feeling back into his feet. He would not forget that journey in a hurry.

He was sorry to leave Killin, and hoped to go back in the summer, but it would be good to be home for Christmas. There would be no snow in Oban, and he was beginning to think that 'white Christmases' were over-rated.

3

Lochgilphead – Ardrishaig – Inveraray

Iain's first move came in January, 1936, and was a direct exchange of posts with Hugh Davidson, who had served his apprenticeship in Lochgilphead and was also due for his first posting. Through a friend he found 'digs' with Mrs MacEwan who had a flat in McLullich's building in Lorne Street. She was a widow in her sixties whose husband had been a clerk in the office of a local lawyer, but who had died in the dreadful 'flu epidemic of 1919. Her first language was Gaelic and she was a strict sabbatarian, but his fellow lodger, Sandy Taylor, explained that her beliefs were of a very literal order.

'I'm sure she's much more afraid of the gossip of the neighbours than the fires of hell,' he said. 'We are not allowed to play the gramophone on Sundays, but it's all right to put on the wireless so long as it is a man talking and not a musical instrument. I've pointed out that this means we are denied the glories of Bach, who was surely making music for the Lord, but can listen to dirty jokes, so long as we keep the volume down. It doesn't make any kind of sense, but she won't budge.'

Sandy had a large collection of classical records and Iain received a thorough education in music during his years there. It was a happy household and 'Cewan' looked after her boys well, in spite of their teasing. After his first day in the new office, the three of them sat together around the kitchen table listening to the famous announcement: *'The King's life is moving peacefully to its close.'*

When he had gone in to the office that morning the first thing he had seen was the familiar red thatch of Donald Cormack who had been promoted to Lochgilphead shortly before. 'Hello, it's yourself. He's in his room. That door,' was his laconic greeting, but he added a huge grin which made the newcomer feel welcome. Donald was still accountant/teller but this was a much busier office, and there was a fully trained ledger clerk, Robert Durno Mackay, and Iain himself, as well as Mr Munro, the manager.

The business came from the County Office, the County Engineer's department and the Police Headquarters; the Argyll and Bute Mental Hospital; the vehicle licensing office; and a large hinterland of small farmers, as well as a handful of hotels and, of course, the shops.

Like Tarbert and Killin, but not Oban, there was a large bank house attached to the office and, in this case, an enormous garden. Mr Munro was not himself an enthusiastic gardener, but he had a passion for order and felt driven to keep the garden tidy. As his wife was an invalid and his daughter had all her spare time, when she was not at work, devoted to the care of her mother and the running of the household, he felt it incumbent upon him to take charge of the garden – just another job to be fitted in as and when he could. But his disappearances into the garden could be disconcerting as Iain soon discovered. A customer came in and asked to see the agent and Iain went into the room where he had just presented himself. It was empty!

Puzzled, he whispered to Donald, 'He's not there!'

'Go and look in the garden,' said Donald out of the side of his mouth. Sure enough, there he was pruning his roses, and all was well.

'How did he get there? I was speaking to him five minutes ago,' he asked.

'Through the window – it's low enough and it's a habit he has,' said the imperturbable Donald.

The next place to look would have been the garage. Mr Munro was the first manager Iain had known who owned his own car and used it regularly to visit customers in the outlying areas. On a good day he had a habit of slipping through the window of his room behind the office and setting off for a run to Ford or Tayvallich and coming back with pocketfuls of cash and cheques.

'That's from Ford Hotel,' he would say, 'and that's from Craigie's garage, and that's from Neil Vernal. Oh, and will you send cash for this, and send Mrs Gillies a new cheque book.'

There was a busy auction mart, and most farmers came in to town only on market days and term days. Some came by car and many by bus, but Johnnie McArthur came in from Danna in a pony and trap and tied the horse to the railings outside the bank. As soon as he entered, Mr Cormack muttered in an aside to Iain, 'You'd better nip outside and watch that horse doesn't work itself loose. It's been known to happen!' The pony was well trained and could be relied upon to take Johnny home after a long session with his cronies in the Stag Hotel.

One of Iain's favourite customers was old Archie Gillies from Arichonan, near Tayvallich. He had an impressive white beard, and was a bachelor who had spent his working life as a shepherd in

Australia and had then retired to his native Argyll to live with his nephews. His native language had been Gaelic and he still spoke with a rich highland accent, in spite of his years abroad. He came to the bank one morning still fuming after a row with his nephews.

'Lazy good-for-nothings, waiting for a bus to take them to Lochgilphead! When I was their age I used to go twenty-three miles on horseback every morning, just to collect the mail!'

All farm servants were paid half-yearly in May and November. They went into the bank with their cheques and drew enough to last for the next six months, leaving a small amount for savings. Very few of them bothered with cheque books.

There were only two banks in the town, the Union Bank and the Clydesdale. So notes from other banks, brought in by the shops and hotels, tended to mount up as they couldn't be re-issued. This was dealt with by the monthly remittance.

Once a month, a clerk from the Greenock office loaded into the purser's office of the MacBrayne steamer locked, black, tin boxes bearing a new supply of notes and coin for the Rothesay, Tarbert, Ardrishaig and Lochgilphead offices. Meanwhile, each of the local offices packed their surplus notes into a similar box and a clerk carried it down to meet the steamer. The Greenock clerk had a green card establishing his identity, and the others had similar orange cards.

'And there we would be, standing at the foot of the gang-way waving our orange cards, looking for a chap waving a green card. Then we would do a quick swap and Bert and I would get on the bus. Bert would drop off at the Ardrishaig office and the bus would stop for me outside our office. We were probably carrying hundreds of pounds, but no-one took any notice. I suppose the boxes looked no more interesting than the black box carried by the bus conductor,' said Iain.

Bank of England notes were dealt with differently. At that time these were large white notes printed on one side only, in black. The only difference between them was the amount, so they were very easily confused, especially in the pubs when the drink was flowing freely. The teller had to be always on the lookout for mistakes in lodgements of English notes but, fortunately, they were used fairly infrequently.

These notes were never re-issued. The customer was asked to sign them on the back and when two or three hundred pounds worth had been accumulated, two lists of the numbers were made in copying ink and these lists were recorded, using the letter-press.

The notes were then cut carefully down the middle and half was sent with one list in a registered envelope to 62 Cornhill, London. A separate letter of notification was sent in the same post. The following day the process was repeated with the other half. Iain often wondered whose job it was to match them up. (As a note is merely a 'promise to pay', once it is in the hands of the bank who issued it, it is really meaningless, and the Bank of England would lose nothing but the printing costs by scrapping these notes.)

As in Oban, Iain's spare time was spent on the golf course and with the local drama club. The SCDA competitions were a great feature in Scottish life in the thirties. The movement had been growing rapidly since the mid-twenties and by 1937 there were more than a thousand amateur groups throughout Scotland. The Scottish newspapers all carried weekly columns featuring the activities of the clubs and they gave the results of the competitions as today they record the football results.

Joe Corrie was one Scottish writer whose work became widely known through the one-act plays written for these competitions. His work carried a strong socialist critique of prevailing social conditions and it was through playing the son in the Lochgilphead club's production of his play, *The Darkness*, a tragic play about mining, that Iain got an opportunity to play on the stage of the Lyric Theatre in Glasgow.

'However, before we could do that,' Iain recalled, 'the club had to devise a means to transport its flats, furniture and properties to Rothesay to compete in the first round. In the end we decided to take the whole lot with us on the steamer.'

Having won there, they hired a bus to take the entire cast and stage crew, plus flats and equipment, to Glasgow for the Divisional finals. They fared no better there than the Oban club had done earlier, for the competition in the west of Scotland was intense, and some of the Glasgow clubs reached a near professional standard.

The 9-hole golf course was just across a side road from the bank, and it was while standing on the first tee that Iain received the telegram telling him that the 1937 bank clerks' strike had been cancelled.

Wages were not as high as they should have been, but there was an ascending scale which allowed the bank's employees to feel that they were making some progress year by year. When the scale rise was cancelled for the second year running, the staff had had enough and the Scottish Bankers Association called their members out on strike. Iain was the local correspondent of the Association, and he had no difficulty in persuading the rest of the staff to join him in the strike, in spite of Mr Munro's blandishments. The banks had not believed that their staffs would actually carry out their threat, but in the event they hurriedly agreed to restore the scale increments. The staff had hoped for more, but settled for what they could get.

Iain opened the telegram and groaned with dismay.

'What's up?' asked his partners, who were all bank staff.

'The strike's off! We've got our increments. Now we'll have to go back in!' he replied.

'Pity you opened it. Can't you pretend you didn't?' asked Robert Mackay.

'Hardly,' said Donald, 'Mr Munro can see us from the house window and, in any case, he'll have had word and he'll know fine where we are.' There was nothing for it but to troop disconsolately back to work. It seemed a waste of a lovely day.

They really felt cheated. The banks opened on Saturdays at that time and the golf course was closed on Sundays. So a morning on the golf course was a rare treat.

When Iain arrived in Lochgilphead, Ardrishaig was a separate two-man office. One of the economies made by the bank at this time was that of putting two nearby branches under one manager, each still retaining its separate identity. As a result of this policy, Mr Munro took over at Ardrishaig. The Ardrishaig manager was sent to Keith, and Iain was sent to help Bert Arbuckle, the accountant, to run the Ardrishaig office.

'Compared with Lochgilphead,' he said, 'Ardrishaig was a cushy number, and that first summer I used to enjoy walking home from Ardrishaig along the canal banks. Even then, I'd arrive home while the Lochgilphead staff were still working.'

When Iain went there the Ardrishaig office had no telephone, which meant that it was not easy for the two branches to communicate. When Bert was on holiday, Lochgilphead sent relief if they could, but they were so busy, and Ardrishaig was so quiet, that this help was grudged and very often he had to manage single-handed. On one such occasion an American tourist came into the office to cash his dollar traveller's cheques, and Iain did not know the rate, but he was a quick-thinker!

'I'm afraid I will have to get the most up-to-date rate of exchange from our overseas department,' he said. 'Could you perhaps take a look round the village and I'll have it for you in half-an-hour?'

As soon as the man had gone, he locked the front door and nipped round the back to the grocer's next door. 'Can I use your telephone? It's urgent,' he pleaded.

'Donald,' he begged, as soon as he was through, 'can you give me today's dollar rate – fast? I've an American coming back any minute!'

Donald looked it up, and Iain was back behind the counter, with all the details at his fingertips, when the customer returned, and was able to cash his cheque with ease.

The American was pleased. 'You know,' he drawled, 'Ah really am impressed by the service you get from the Scottish banks – even in the sticks!'

After a year of this easy life, Iain was moved back to Lochgilphead, where he was needed to go to Inveraray once a week to help Mr Macpherson, the manager, with the sub-branch at Strachur.

This was quite a performance. Each Thursday morning he caught the nine o'clock bus to Inveraray and as soon as he arrived in the office two bags were packed, one containing cash and the other the ledger, spare cheque books and the necessary stationery. These were hauled down to the slip where an open motor-boat was waiting to take them across Loch Fyne to St Catherine's.

There, a car hired from the hotel would take them down the road to Strachur, but they made slow progress as they stopped at various small businesses along the way as a matter of course. At any of these they might be told, 'Mrs So-and-so wants to see you. She'll meet you at the road-end.' Or they might be flagged down at the gate of any cottager who happened to want to cash a cheque or pay money into an account.

Eventually, they arrived at a small bungalow, where a room was reserved for their use. Notices establishing that this was now a bank were fixed on the wall and manager and ledger clerk took up their posts at tables at either end of the room. A steady flow of customers queued outside the door and were admitted one at a time. Too bad if it was raining, though a few could take shelter in the entrance hall. Perhaps, as many of them were forestry workers waiting to cash their pay cheques and were dressed for the weather, they wouldn't be bothered by a drop of rain.

When they finally returned to Inveraray, Mr Macpherson was invariably first out of the boat, scrambling hastily up the slip and calling over his shoulder, 'Come on, come on. I'm late for my dinner!' Since Mrs Macpherson knew perfectly well when to expect them back, his dinner was unlikely to be spoiled but, no doubt, his stomach was less adaptable. Iain didn't care one way or the other: one of the perks of these Thursday excursions was that he had his dinner in the George Hotel – at the bank's expense.

He regularly did relief at Inveraray to let other members of staff have their holidays. Almost the first day he was on the counter there, a tramp-like figure entered the bank. Polite by nature, Iain greeted him courteously and was surprised when his greeting was returned in an educated accent. Though he found the customer's scribbled signature indecipherable, Iain saw no reason to refuse to cash his small cheque. When he had left, the girl clerk asked in some amusement, 'Did you know who that was?'

'No,' replied Iain, 'but he seemed all right.'

'I should say he was,' she laughed. 'That was the Duke of Argyll!'

The tenth Duke of Argyll was an elderly bachelor who despised all modern innovations. He rode round the village on an ancient bicycle, and when the telephone company had sought permission to erect an exchange on his land, he had refused point-blank. They had had to resort to a plot of land quite some distance outside the village which was owned by his sister, Lady Elspeth Campbell.

The whole town had been rebuilt by an earlier Duke as a 'new town' at the time of the Enlightenment. When the English nobility were having their estates landscaped by Capability Brown and others, the Scots lairds, finding their landscapes less tractable, no doubt, had resorted instead to building model villages. Inveraray is perhaps the most notable example.

It had been the County town in earlier days, had a well-known grammar school and was the seat of the Sheriff. The whole bloody history of the Scottish clans can be read in the annals of Inveraray. In the garden of the bank house there was a stone memorial, tall enough to be seen from the passing bus over the garden wall, marking the spot where a number of rebels had been hanged at the time of the Stuart uprisings. The Dukes of Argyll were staunch Protestants and took the side of 'Butcher Cumberland' against the 'rebels' who, like their leaders, remained faithful to the Catholic cause. (The monument has since been removed to the castle policies.)

A more cheerful memory of Inveraray was the annual launching of Mr Macpherson's boat. This sizeable small yacht was stored (with its sails and mast removed) in a storeroom belonging to the bank, on the far side of the front door. One morning the local joiners arrived to take out the window of this room, and once that had been done Mr Macpherson could be heard shouting to his four sons, 'Right! Peter, James, John. Where's Alexander?'

At this point, every able-bodied man who was available became involved in the tricky business of easing the boat through the window and on to a specially constructed trailer positioned in the street outside. Once it was safely lashed to the trailer, it was taken down to the slip to be launched.

The whole process was repeated at the end of the sailing season. Safely in the bank, it was not only secure, but readily available for Mr Macpherson to carry out those mysterious processes which keep sailors happy during the winter months.

Iain did not see it relaunched, however. In Autumn 1938, the bank had a major shake-up and all the unmarried staff found themselves on the move. He was sent to Alva, in Clackmannanshire, his father's home county, and his predecessor there was sent to St Margaret's Hope in Orkney. They never knew the reason for this. It was simply a case of 'Mine is not to reason why...' For a young man with no ties, it made life interesting.

4

Alva – Preparing for War

Alva was a small town about eight miles from Stirling, lying at the foot of the Ochil Hills. There were three of these small burghs, the other two being Tillicoultry and Dollar, and together they were known as 'the Hillfoots'. An English visitor tried to argue that it should be 'the Hillfeet' but he was soon disabused of that idea. There was an old saying in the district,

'Ye can aye tell a Hillfitter – but ye canna tell him onything!'

The dialect was quite different from the soft Highland version of Scots that Iain had grown up with, and it was some time before he was quite sure that he understood what his new landlady, Mrs Westland, was saying.

At breakfast the first morning she told him, 'There's nae hurry, that knock's fornent!' If she hadn't nodded at the clock at the same time, he couldn't possibly have guessed that she was telling him that the kitchen clock was fast. 'Ye see ah'm wantin' a finga,' she added, and proceeded to tell him a long story, the gist of which seemed to be that she had lost her finger while working in the mill when she was jist a bit lassie.

In many ways it was a different world. Mrs Westland was a widow who had brought up a son and two daughters in a council house about a hundred yards from the station. The son had left home to become a fireman in Glasgow and his room had been occupied by a series of Union Bank clerks. It was taken for granted that he would stay with her as, 'Mrs Westland aye teks the laddie frae the bank.'

They were a friendly family, and within six months Iain had attended the weddings of all three of Mrs Westland's children. The elder daughter was married in the Johnston Hall in Alva, Jim in an hotel in Tillicoultry, and the younger daughter opted for a Church of Scotland service in Alva. The house was in a continual turmoil of preparation and Iain quite enjoyed his role as a participator on the fringe of all this excitement.

Jim confided in him that, 'It teks a deal of money tae get marriet, nooadays. Ye ken ye canna set up hoose on less than a hunner punn.' It had taken Jim a long time to amass a hundred pounds, but he wouldn't have thought it proper to propose until he was nearing his target. Respectability was important and starting off in debt was not to be considered. Some people might have considered setting up home on hire purchase, but in those unchancy times it would have been thought irresponsible – what happened if you lost your job? Jim Westland had been brought up respectable and Iain developed a great respect for his widowed landlady.

There were two banks in Alva, the other being a small branch of the Commercial Bank still operating under a lawyer-agent, helped by a staff of two, but the Union Bank had by far the bigger business and the staff were run off their feet. This meant that it was a case of 'all hands to the pump' and Alva was by far the most unconventional office that Iain had come across. Normally areas of responsibility were strictly delineated, and the man appointed to be in charge of the cash, whether he was a straightforward teller or an accountant/teller, was wholly responsible for the cash and was the only member of staff to serve at the counter. If the cash didn't balance it was his responsibility, so he would take a dim view of anyone else even touching it. When the teller was away, someone else took over the cash and he was then responsible; if a second till had to be opened, the person operating it was responsible and the cash in that till was balanced separately. What you never did was to have several members of staff operating the same till – but it happened at Alva.

The manager, Mr Walker was like no other manager Iain had known. He had a short-lived but fiery temper and he worked like one possessed. Normally he took charge of the counter himself, but of course, in a busy office, he often had to leave it to deal with customers privately in his office. In those circumstances either the accountant, Charlie Dougall, would take over, or if he was up to the eyes, as he frequently was, Iain soon realised that it was up to him to fill the breach. He had never worked so hard in his life, but he enjoyed himself immensely as he felt he was part of a team who were all pulling their weight.

Mr Walker was not well and frequently had to take time off to attend a physiotherapist for treatment which, of course, meant even more work for Charlie and Iain. But when he was in the office, the boss worked as hard as the others and carried the responsibility for the branch as well. Iain felt he was entitled to his occasional outbursts of temper.

'I had a spell in Inveraray, myself, when I was younger,' he told Iain, 'and my wife comes from Kintyre.' So he was aware of the adjustments his new clerk was having to make. All in all it was a happy office.

There being only two banks in the burgh, mixed notes accumulated as in other small places. In Alva this meant that Charlie and Iain arrived at the office at 8.30am on Thursday mornings and picked up the surplus notes before catching the bus to Alloa, which was about four miles distant. In the Alloa office they met up with other clerks from Tillicoultry and Kincardine-on-Forth as well as the Alloa staff. The Alloa office took their mixed notes and replaced them with Union Bank notes and, if necessary, they were able to replenish their supplies of silver and copper. As all the banks had branches in Alloa, the Alloa staff were able to dispose of all these notes at their local note exchange. These opportunities for meeting with colleagues were friendly social occasions at one level, but they meant that, when these young men finally acquired a branch of their own, they had built up a wide network of contacts in other branches.

The business at Alva was totally different from that in any of the branches that Iain had worked in before. 'You see,' he said, 'the customers in Argyll were essentially rural, whatever their occupation, and the isolation of Highland communities led to a closely knit, but geographically limited, social life. The business at Alva was different altogether. For a start, it was more industrial: there was a large spinning mill, two tweed factories and several firms that manufactured knitted garments. On top of that, many local men were miners working at a coal pit not far from the town; others were printers, as there was a large printing works, so there was plenty of trade union activity. There was none of that in Argyll; the bankers' strike fairly raised the eyebrows!'

Instead of a large number of independent shop-keepers, he noticed that the Alva Co-operative Society Ltd seemed to run nearly all the retail business in the town. They had two grocers, men's and women's outfitters, chemists, coalmerchants, a fishmonger, a greengrocer and a furniture shop. (As Charlie said, 'Whatever you want – you'll find it in the Co-op.') It is not surprising to learn that the area regularly sent a Labour member to Parliament.

As the bank held the Co-op account, they were kept pretty busy dealing with the takings of all these businesses, but they held most of the industrial accounts as well. It really was a very busy office, and so Mr Walker was desperate to get another member of staff. Eventually, in the spring following Iain's arrival in the branch, Mr Walker heard that the inspectors were in Stirling, and when he was told to meet them in Stirling for lunch, he hoped that, at last, something might be about to happen. He came back overjoyed. 'We have a new apprentice starting on Monday,' he told the others, 'He's the son of the manager at Bridge of Allan, so he should have some idea.'

His delight was short-lived. On the Friday before the boy was about to start, he got a phone call from Glasgow telling him that there was an emergency in Doune where a member of staff had taken ill, and Mr Rattray was to go there to help out until further notice. 'But I can't do without him,' he pleaded, 'we are up to the eyes!'

'That will be no problem,' he was assured, 'you will have Mr Flockhart starting on Monday.'

The poor man tried to argue that a boy who was just starting was hardly able to do the work of a fully trained and qualified member of staff, but he might as well have saved his breath. He was entitled to a staff of three. He had a staff of three. That was it. He was furious, but there was not a thing he could do about it, and Iain started in Doune on the Monday morning.

Doune was a two-man office where the agent was also the Town Clerk. On the Monday morning, as soon as Iain had been shown the ropes, the agent said, 'Right then, I'm off to see the Provost. Expect me when you see me!' And Iain was left to run the place single-handed. This was a regular occurrence. Even so, after Alva, it was a dawdle! There was very little business and, after catching a bus to Stirling and another to Alva, he would still reach his digs before Alva staff stopped working. Sometimes he went in to lend a hand, but not invariably – he had other irons in the fire.

Although the town was near an 18-hole golf course at Schaw Park (where the bank staffs organised competitions for staff from surrounding offices), a nine-hole burgh course and a football club, Iain found that he could travel easily into Stirling. 'My aunt and uncle lived there,' he said, 'and I had always spent a month of my school holidays with them – so all the time I was in Alva I took them to the pictures every week. It was the least I could do, and I looked forward to it.' By this time, too, his sister was nursing at the Children's Hospital in Glasgow, and on Saturday or Sunday afternoons he was able to take her out for a meal and perhaps to visit one of the theatres. Never before had he had such a choice of entertainment, from first-division football to the latest films and live theatre, and he made the most of it.

Every month An Comunn Gaidhealach (the Gaelic Society) held meetings in Stirling, and these were attended by Highlanders from all over the surrounding district, whether they were fluent Gaelic speakers or not. Everyone knew someone you knew back home, and the chances of meeting someone from Oban High School were great. But it wasn't at An Comunn that he met Miss Forbes; that was at a meeting of the Scottish National Party. He wasn't a member, but he was curious, and attending public meetings could be an entertainment in itself and a cheap one at that! There had been two Nationalist parties, but these had recently amalgamated and the new body opened a branch in Stirling and advertised its meetings. There were about a dozen people there, and soon after he arrived, a young woman tapped him on the shoulder and said, 'I think I taught you French at Oban High School.' He was astonished at how young she looked.

'They were a pretty innocuous bunch,' he told me later, 'and they didn't do much. They just sat around drinking tea and talking, but no-one took them seriously and they were regarded as a bunch of eccentrics.' He wasn't hooked at the time but like many other Scots he sees the SNP rather differently now.

He also went to a meeting of the Peace Pledge Union which was addressed by George MacLeod, founder of the Iona Community, and this was much more to his liking. He had been a pacifist as long as he could remember, though it wasn't a thing he ever spoke about while he was growing up. Born in 1914, one of his earliest memories had been of being taken by his father to see the troops coming home after the 1914-18 war. 'Everyone had flags to wave, most of them Union Jacks, but I remember my father insisted on a Scottish Lion Rampant for me,' he said. 'Men came back disabled and blind, and Mrs Kennedy had lost two sons in the same week. Almost every family had some story of tragedy and in a small place like Oban, these stories were known.'

In school, male teachers who had fought in the war were embittered at the pointlessness of the slaughter and, repeatedly, had impressed on their pupils, 'This must never happen again.' Most boys shrugged it off, but with Iain it had stuck and he knew there was no way he could kill another person, just because he was on the wrong side. He couldn't kill another person – full stop!

The master who ran the Cadet Corps in the school put a Balmoral on Iain's head one day and said, 'There, now, that suits you just fine. How about joining the cadets?'

'No, thank you, sir,' he replied firmly.

'Oh, come on, you like games – you'd enjoy it,' the master argued.

'No, sir,' was the stubborn answer. The master recognised inflexibility when he saw it and let it go, but he must have been puzzled, as the boy was normally an easy-going and compliant pupil. Iain could have explained that he was already in the Scouts and that would have provided excuse enough, but that wasn't the real reason so he wouldn't give it. He just didn't want to learn how to kill people, but he felt you could hardly tell a master that, so he just said, 'No,' and stuck to it.

He admitted later, 'It was a pity in a way – the Balmoral was a great improvement on those awful Scout hats they made us wear with our kilts!'

As he progressed through his training he realised that war was becoming more than a possibility and he knew he would refuse to fight when the time came, but meantime there was nothing to be done about it. He remembers driving his Father's car up to Ardrishaig at the time of the Abyssinian crisis and thinking, 'They are going to fight, but I won't. I might get killed, and if so, so be it, but I am not going to kill someone else.'

The first time he really discussed it was with Dochie MacDougall in Lochgilphead. Dochie was a character. He was about Iain's own age, but unemployed most of the time, although occasionally he got a job unloading the puffers that brought coal to Miller's Bridge. Physically he was tough and he looked it, so it would be an understatement to say that Iain was surprised when Dochie approached him one day and asked, 'Excuse me. Can you explain to me what "the fiduciary issue of the Bank of England" means, please?'

'Well, yes, I suppose I could – but not now, I'm late for the office. Why on earth do you want to know that, anyway?' he replied.

'Just interest. Look, are you doing anything tonight? Could we meet at Capocci's corner, say seven o'clock? It's a great night for a walk.' Dochie suggested.

'OK, but better make it half-past – I'm never sure when we'll get finished, and I'll have to get my tea and get out of these clothes,' Iain agreed, and that was the start of an unusual friendship.

He soon discovered that Dochie was a glutton for learning and would cultivate anyone who had knowledge of his current area of interest. At that time he was into economics, and Iain was newly qualified in banking, and so was likely to be able to help him. Another of his friends was an expert in astronomy and yet another knew all about local history, and so on. Dochie's interests were wide and deep. The two young men became friends and Iain soon discovered that he was learning more from Dochie than Dochie was learning from him. But they didn't agree on politics. Dochie was a committed Marxist. Iain had been brought up in a Liberal household, but while his views, such as they were, could have been described as left of centre, they were based largely on the Highlander's dislike of the landlords. He hated the idea of being dominated by people in London, who knew nothing of the lives of those who lived on vast tracts of barely populated land owned by 'lairds' who spent their time and their money in the South. He had a humanitarian concern for the underdog rather than an ideological credo. In any case, he thought Marx's economic theory was faulty.

Many Marxists were opposed to fighting in support of a capitalist regime, but Dochie took the view that Fascism had to be opposed at all costs, while Iain personalised the issue. 'That's all very well, but when you drop your bomb how do you know it's going to kill Fascists? It's far more likely to kill women and children who neither know nor care a fig about politics.'

It didn't affect their friendship and, though the difference in opinion added spice to their talk, they simply honed their arguments against the challenge of the other. If they got too heated, there were plenty of other things to discuss.

By the time Iain moved to Alva, it was becoming evident that war was imminent, and when he returned from his spell at Doune, the bank was already beginning to make preparations. Lists were made of the names of all the accounts and safe custody deposit holders, in duplicate, using indelible pencils and carbon paper. This took several nights. On the Sunday morning that war was declared, they worked all day adding figures to the names, showing the balances at the close of business on the Saturday. The carbon copies were exchanged for those of another branch in a different part of the country. When these lists were received they were placed, unopened, in the strongroom and were to be used only if the other branch received a direct hit – in which case the essential records would be readily available. Thereafter, each day a carbon copy of 'the clean cash book' was sent to the partner branch. After each quarterly balance complete new lists were sent.

The black-out had already started when Iain and Charlie went out for a meal that Sunday night, before returning to finish their mammoth task. On the way back, they met two local girls and stopped to chaff them. One of the girls was fretting because she could see a chink of light showing under the blind of the shop on the corner. 'That's terrible,' she said, 'it's just asking the Germans to bomb us.'

Iain still remembers his sarcastic reply, 'Oh, yes, I can just see old Hitler sitting back there in Berlin and telling Goering, "Never mind London or Glasgow or Edinburgh – there's a place in the Ochils called Alva. Now that's the place you have to knock out first!'" Truth to tell, none of them knew what to expect, but they were all taken by surprise by the long period in which life seemed to go on much as before, except for the black-out.

During this period of 'the phoney war', the people who were most affected were the men who had volunteered for the Territorials in peace-time, and their families. These men were called up at once, and many bank clerks were among them. One result of this was a sudden depletion in staff, and though women were being recruited to replace them, they took time to train and, meantime, the bank issued instructions that no-one was to volunteer for any kind of full-time service on any account. The assumption was that anyone who did would lose his position with the bank permanently, but it wasn't exactly spelt out. That put paid to any idea of joining the fire service or becoming an ambulance driver or something of the sort. In any case, Iain would have felt that it was a cowardly way of dodging the issue.

Meanwhile, like the rest of his age group, he worked harder than ever and waited to see what would happen. Men were being ordered to register in batches, starting with the eighteen year olds. It would be a while before they got to Iain and, as he had already made up his mind to refuse, there was nothing for it but to get on with life in the bank – and wait.

5

Leith – The Bank in Wartime

Earlier in its history, the Union Bank, which had its headquarters in Glasgow, had taken over a smaller bank with impressive headquarters in Edinburgh. Thus it came about that the bank had Head Offices in both cities. The directors met in Glasgow, but the Edinburgh Head Office retained a certain amount of autonomy. This meant that if a member of staff was being moved into the Edinburgh area, he was transferred first to the Head Office in Edinburgh and they allocated him to a branch.

It was early in 1940 that Iain was told to report to George Street, Edinburgh, the following week. Realising that it would be difficult, and probably too expensive, to get into one of the Edinburgh golf clubs, he took his clubs home to Oban that week-end. Then, having reduced his possessions to the contents of one case, he set off for the capital city.

On arrival, the first thing to do was to report to the messenger at the door. (The messengers were members of the staff who performed many of the functions now undertaken by security firms.) He was soon joined by two other new arrivals and they were all briefed by the fatherly messenger. 'Right! Which of you is Mr Rattray? You? Well you're going to Leith.' The others were also told their destinations, before the messenger added, 'Remember, you don't let on that you know where you're going, let it come as a surprise. I'm just telling you now so that you won't feel so nervous when you go in.'

With that, Iain was ushered into the imposing office of Mr Hall, the Edinburgh manager. This gentleman wore a frock coat and an upright stiff collar and, after the briefest of exchanges, told him formally that he was to report to Bernard Street, Leith, and gave him a letter of introduction to the branch manager. Then, in a fleeting moment of humanity, he added, 'If you just walk down to the corner of Princes Street, you can get a tram that will take you right there.' The interview was over.

Bernard Street, Leith, was on a busy corner site not far from the docks, and the minute he entered Iain realised that this was an exceptionally busy office. Mr Gorrie, the manager, wasted no time, and after the briefest of greetings, said abruptly, 'Right, Mr Rattray, you'll take charge of both ledgers, and the sooner you can get started the better!'

He then took him into the office where he was introduced to Mr Corrie, the accountant; Mr Dickie, the teller; and to Miss Thorburn, a lady in her forties who had come into the bank during the first war as a 'temporary' member of staff and was still there. She was extremely knowledgeable and efficient and Iain said later, 'I'd been in the bank about nine years by that time, and I was earning more than she was after twenty-five years, and she was good! I thought it was most unfair.'

The Port of Leith was a very large burgh in its own right, until it was merged with Edinburgh after the First World War. 'And most of us didn't like that, Mr Rattray. We didn't like it at all!' said Miss Thorburn. The Union Bank had two branches there, but the Commercial Bank had four! It was very much a trading centre and

Iain found that most of the bank's customers were large companies. Mr Gorrie met from time to time with the directors of these firms, but it was the staff who were dealt with at the counter. Altogether customer relations were far more formal and impersonal than in the smaller branches he had worked in before. To some extent this applied to the staff as well. 'You know,' he said, 'I thought it was weird. We all got on well together at work, but when the doors closed we all went our separate ways to different parts of the city. I knew practically nothing about the private lives of the folk I worked with.' It is just not possible to separate one's private life from one's home life to that extent in a village or small burgh, and he found it very odd at first. He found it equally odd that everyone in Leith from the highest to the lowest seemed to travel to work by tramcar. (The company car had not yet been dreamt of!)

'You should have seen all these city gents, with their stiff collars and bowler hats and umbrellas and briefcases, boarding the same trams as dockers and typists. Members of the same firm, travelling on the same tram, didn't necessarily sit together. You would have thought they didn't even know each other. It was all very strange to a boy from the country,' he said.

It was one of the few offices that could issue drafts in foreign currency. One of the differences this made was that three signatories were required to operate the accounts in order to accommodate the requirements of some foreign banks. Most Scottish branches asked for one, but Leith Branch, which served a busy port, did a great deal of overseas business. Both France and Norway had consulates in Leith. Most of their customers were in the import/export business, and among these were the Ben Line (whose offices where in what had been the bank house which occupied the floors above the bank), and the Federation of Icelandic Co-operative Societies. They had a customer in the Faroe Isles and many from Scandinavia. Indeed, there were so many Scandinavians in Leith that they had their own church, the Norse Kirk. In addition, there were several light engineering firms, two huge flour mills and a firm of whisky distillers who exported mainly to Southern and Central America.

The outbreak of war had an immediate impact on almost all of these businesses. The Leith, Hull and Hamburg Shipping Company had a great deal of trouble with the censors, as the word 'Hamburg' immediately aroused suspicion, so they changed their name to Currie Line Ltd. When the Germans invaded Denmark and Norway, the sudden deterioration in the situation had an enormous effect on Leith, as so many firms had dealings with those countries. Mr Gorrie had an anxious time taking affected customers into Edinburgh for meetings with government representatives to try to sort out the horrendous consequences for firms who had been heavily involved in the occupied countries and were now facing disaster.

'We knew all this was going on, of course, but dealing with it was far above my level of competence at that time,' he said. 'I was too busy trying to make sure the two ledgers were immaculate and balanced. Two minor inaccuracies or smudges would be pointed out and forgiven, but three warranted a call to Mr Gorrie's office for a dressing down!' Fortunately that happened rarely. The war might be pressing, and the bombs starting to fall but standards must be maintained!

Actually, the bombing of Leith was never on the same scale as it was at Clydebank, but that was no consolation to those who were injured or bereaved, and the danger was real enough to ensure that precautions were taken seriously. As has been said, the bank stood on a corner site, and consequently had windows on two walls. At night, it was Iain's responsibility to bar the outer door on the inside, put up and bar the shutters on the insides of all the windows. When everyone else had left, he would exit through a hidden door in a cupboard in the manager's office, lock it, and pass down a short corridor to an unobtrusive single door on to the street to which he held one of the keys.

When the siren went, Iain immediately barred the front outside door and started to put up the shutters while Mr Corrie and Miss Thorburn shepherded the customers into the manager's room, which doubled as an air-raid shelter. The outer wall was permanently sandbagged from floor to ceiling, covering the only window, and by the time Iain joined them there might be as many as fifteen people in that small room, which had a high roof, but no ventilation. Meanwhile, the teller put all the money in the safe, locked it, and took up a seat in front of it – a very literal interpretation of the term 'solely responsible for the cash!'

Thus the teller was the only one who was able to hear what was going on outside and it was he who, when the all clear sounded, opened the door of the inner office and announced, 'You can come out now. That's the siren.'

Iain had, after spending a few weeks with a 'rather posh' acquaintance of Miss Thorburn's, found digs with Mrs Gilbert, who ran a boarding house in Leopold Place. If the siren went during the night, the six male residents joined Mrs Gilbert and her invalid husband and daughter in the sandbagged family sitting room in the basement. These were quite cheerful occasions, as one of the residents was an old navy man who would produce a bottle of rum and add a large tot to the cups of tea that Mrs Gilbert had ready for them.

As Mr Gilbert was suffering from the effects of being shell-shocked in the First World War, the raids must have been particularly trying for him. However, the lodgers were a friendly and cheerful bunch and did their best to turn these occasions into a party. They were never in acute danger, but one bomb dropped within quarter of a mile, and an anti-aircraft shell hit the fire station across the road. Later Iain said, 'The noise of the trams kept me awake for the first fortnight, but I can't say I lost much sleep through the air-raids.'

Nevertheless, as the raids became more frequent and 'pill-boxes' began to appear at strategic junctions (the first Iain saw was at the West end of Princes Street), the powers that be in Edinburgh Head Office decided that further precautions were necessary to protect the cash. So each night all the notes were taken to the vaults under the George Street office. As soon as the ledger and the cash were balanced, Iain and the teller collected and bagged the notes and took them on the tram into town. The following morning they would be found standing outside the vaults, waiting for the time lock to operate at 9am so that they could retrieve their bag.

This meant that the job of locking up the branch had to be devolved on to the tiny shoulders of Isobel Girdwood, who had joined the bank straight from school and looked as if she should be still in the first form! In fact she was an excellent clerkess, definitely 'a find', but when Mr Gorrie first caught sight of her he said in horror, 'Good God, Mr Corrie – they've sent us a *child!*'

Though most of the business was with big firms they did, of course, have a number of smaller and personal accounts. One of the latter was that of a single lady, Sarah Smith*, who Iain imagined must be verging on the senile. Iain had never met her but, all too frequently, he found himself dealing with her lost cheque books or muddles of one sort or another. However, he had always had a soft spot for old ladies, and as he said, 'I felt quite sorry for the old dear and didn't really mind the trouble she caused. She couldn't help being old and dotty.'

One morning, he looked up from his ledger and there was the most gorgeous girl he had ever seen. To quote Iain, 'She had glorious red hair, looks that would put any film star in the shade, and was dressed like one of the pictures in your fashion magazines.'

She gave him a smile that would have set any young man back on his heels, and Iain was as susceptible as most, and addressed him over the ledger desk. 'I am *so* sorry to trouble you. I can see that you are very busy, but do you think I could speak to the manager?'

---

* not her real name

Iain couldn't move quickly enough. In a second he was round the desk, ready to take her to the North Pole if necessary! 'Of course, I'll take you through. What name shall I say?'

'I've been before,' she said, and she smiled again. 'Tell him it's Sarah Smith.' And he realised this must be his 'dotty old lady'.

Somehow he kept control of his face as he took her through. When he came back Mr Corrie looked up and grunted, 'What on earth has that dizzy dame done now? It must be drastic if she has to come and sweetheart him herself!' She was the daughter of their wealthiest customer!

'I can't remember what she had done,' Iain told me, 'but I'll never forget the shock. Senile indeed! I felt a complete fool!' Later he was taught that a good manager can put a face on every signature. One can see why.

The bank was only five minutes from the docks where ships were being loaded and unloaded incessantly. There was no naval activity as such, but nevertheless security was tight and it was necessary to show a pass to the police sergeant at the gates before one was allowed on to the dock itself. As one of the firms with whom the branch had regular dealings was located on the dock, Iain had a pass which allowed him to visit on behalf of the bank. The first time he used this pass he discovered that the policeman on duty was an ex-pupil of Oban High School who greeted him like a long-lost brother, 'What are you doing now? How long have you been here? I haven't seen you at the Argyllshire Association.'

'Give me time. I've only just arrived. I've read the bits about the Argyllshire Association in the Oban Times, but I hadn't got round to doing anything about it,' said Iain.

'Oh you'll need to join. You'll never get to know anyone if you don't; they're a sticky lot here. I'll propose you and the Inspector will second you.' He scribbled the address. 'Next Monday, then. I'll look out for you.'

In fact, Iain had found the men in his digs very friendly and had already arranged to visit the cinema and the variety theatre with them. He had also bought a season ticket at the Lyceum, which acted as a repertory theatre, so he wasn't as lost and lonely as all that. However, it would be good to meet folk from home who talked his language. He had already been corrected in the office for saying 'Who, Mr Smith?' using the Gaelic idiom, instead of the English, 'Which Mr Smith?' and he rather resented being treated with amusement as a laddie whose accent betrayed the fact that he still 'had heather in his ears.'

The Argyllshire Association was good fun and he was introduced by friends there to *Comunn Tir Nam Beann* which, roughly translated, means The Society of the Land of the Mountains, or The Highland Society. They advertised their social evenings as 'Buntata Sgadan' or 'Tatties and Herring'; and potatoes and herring cooked in oatmeal was, invariably, the supper dish served at these functions. It was at one of these gatherings that someone asked him which church he went to.

'I don't usually go to any,' he admitted.

'Oh, don't worry. I'm not trying to save you,' his new friend laughed. 'It's just that I was going warn you not to go to St Columba's (the best known Gaelic church) as they're all

Sgitheanach and Leodhasach (i.e. from Skye and Lewis). The Argyll folk go to St Oran's and you're sure to find people you know there.'

He had, in fact, read the New Testament through, from beginning to end, more than once during his time in Alva and he couldn't for the life of him see how anyone who professed to be a follower of Jesus could be pro-war. Still, he decided that he would go to St Oran's and see what it was like. In the event he was disappointed with the content of the sermons which seemed to him to oversimplify a very difficult moral dilemma. It was good to meet more old friends but he gave up St Oran's after a few visits. He tried several other denominations but they all seemed to be repeating the same pro-war propaganda and, in spite of the bombing, he still couldn't swallow it.

Mabel and Jessie Mitchell, who had lived next door to the bank in Lochgilphead, had given him the address of their sister Hilda. She had married Gilbert Ludlam, who was a Quaker, and Iain was greeted warmly when he finally visited them. He had met Hilda before and she knew that he was a pacifist and a conscientious objector and would, therefore, have to face a tribunal before he could be excused active service in a fighting unit. She knew how intimidating this could be and immediately offered her support.

'Why don't you come to our Friends' Meeting?' she asked, 'You'll meet plenty of people there who think as you do, and we can give you practical advice that will help you when you go before your tribunal. When is it?'

'I don't know exactly, but it can't be long now. I'm watching for the postman every day,' he replied.

'Well, come next Sunday, and we'll introduce you to everyone. You don't have to join or anything like that, but we can help,' she urged.

'It's kind of you both and I do appreciate it, but no,' he answered quite firmly. 'You see I'm not a Quaker, and it would be wrong of me to give the impression that I'm objecting because I am connected with Friends. They have a good name with the tribunals, I know, but I can't trade on it. I have to sink or swim on my own convictions. I might well end up as a Quaker, but I'll face the music first. Meantime I must keep well away in case I give the wrong impression.' And, though both Hilda and Gilbert did their best, he would not be moved.

When the time came, however, Hilda did go with him to his tribunal, which was held in a Court House in Edinburgh, but he remembers surprisingly little of what must have been quite an ordeal. There were three of them, he said, 'and one of them was a Trade Unionist – I do remember that – but I've no idea who the others were. They asked all the things you would expect and I answered as honestly as I could. I know I emphasised that I was objecting on moral grounds because I thought it was wrong to kill, and that religion didn't come into it. I insisted on that. Then in the end they asked if I would accept non-combatant duties. I didn't really know what they meant by that, but I was prepared to do anything that would help people, so I said that I would. That was all that there was to it really.'

He went for his medical on 1st November 1940 and was quite

surprised that the Medical Officer doing the examination treated him like any other army recruit. He still didn't know what he was going to be told to do. At the end of November he received calling-up papers telling him to report for Non-combatant Corps training at Dingle Vale, Liverpool, in one week's time.

He couldn't get home to see his parents and leave his belongings, unless he could have part of the following Monday morning off, there being no trains from Oban on a Sunday and Mr Gorrie said firmly, 'That's out of the question. Until we get a replacement, you are needed to collect the cash from the vaults.' Fortunately, Mrs Gilbert agreed to keep his things until he could collect them – at least he didn't have to saddle her with his golf clubs!

Mr Gorrie had reported his call-up to Head Office as soon as he knew about it. He was obliged to do so, as he was looking for someone to do the ledgers. This was the first indication his superiors had that they had a 'conchie' in their ranks. They were not amused. The directors met on the Wednesday, his last day. He had to catch the evening train to Liverpool, but he worked up to the very last minute. Around four o'clock Mr Gorrie sent for him. 'I'm really very sorry,' he said, 'but I have to tell you that the directors decided this morning that you are to be suspended, without pay, for the duration.'

6

The Reluctant Soldier

On the train he had time to catch up with himself. The men in the digs had taken him for a last night out the night before and he wondered ruefully if that had been as good an idea as it had seemed at the time. It had been a blow to be told that he was suspended, as other men were getting their service pay made up to the level of their earnings in the bank, but really it was of small consequence. If nothing worse happened before the war was over, he would be lucky indeed. He dozed intermittently until he arrived in Liverpool around six in the morning, in time to experience the tail end of a savage air raid.

He reported to Dingle Vale School and it was rapidly brought home to him just what 'non-combatant service' really meant. He had been recruited into the Non-combatant Corps, a branch of the Pioneer Corps, with this difference – members of the NCC could never be promoted. The Pioneer Corps itself was looked down upon by the rest of the army as the dumping place for those who, for physical, mental or educational reasons, were unfit for anything else. They did routine labouring and maintenance work – but they were soldiers. Thus Iain found himself undergoing the usual admission processes of any army recruit and he was soon introduced to the pleasures of square-bashing, when he was not involved in the more useful work of clearing up the debris after the dreadful air raids that Liverpool was suffering at that time.

On the first night he was one of a party of twenty allocated to a room in a house near Sefton Park. They slept in straw-filled palliasses on the floor, and as they settled themselves down, someone entered the room and called out, 'Any OBs here?' Immediately a group collected and began to talk earnestly in a corner of the room.

Soon afterwards the process was repeated, 'Any EBs here?' At this, most of the rest rushed into another corner.

'What's an OB or an EB?' asked the tall fellow beside him in a comfortingly familiar Glasgow voice.

'I've no idea,' Iain replied, 'but by the sound of them it's something religious – what are you?'

'Me? – I'm a Protestant. The name's Dave Waddell.'

Iain was on familiar ground. In Glasgow there are only two religions – Catholic and Protestant – unless one is an active member of the Free Church, or very committed to another denomination. He knew exactly how to place Dave.

'Mine's Iain Rattray, from Oban. I put NIL on my identity disk.'

'Well, so might I, but I never thought of it. I reckon we're in a minority around here.' He was right in this. The majority were Plymouth Brethren, Open or Exclusive, hence OB or EB. The rest were a mixture of less dogmatic Christians, one or two Jews, a Buddhist, a Marxist, and a bunch who could be described as broadly humanist in outlook. The Brethren kept themselves to themselves and that was how the rest preferred it.

The problem with this set-up, so far as an outsider could understand it at the time, was that the purpose of army training was to turn individuals into cogs in a well-running machine. Those with leadership qualities were encouraged to rise through the ranks to the limit of their ability; the rest were not supposed to think for themselves but were trained to obey orders, instantly and without question. Under fire their lives and the lives of others might depend on it. That, at least, was the theory. Those who resented not being allowed to think for themselves were motivated to strive for promotion but in the NCC there was no promotion (it was made quite clear from the beginning that even a lance-corporal's stripes were not for them) and yet most of them were very intelligent and individualistic. It was a recipe for a mixture of tragedy and farce, but there was more farce than tragedy!

They were moved about the country and living conditions varied. At best they were in normal army huts sleeping on palliasses on two-tier bunks; at worst they were in John o' Gaunt's Tower at Lancaster, sleeping on a flagged floor in mid-winter, with the only light coming from unglazed arrow slits too high to black-out properly, so that they were allowed only a minimal use of candles to prepare themselves for morning parade. The water, of course was icy cold.

Their first move had been to Carlisle, where No.5 company was based, and then they went to Dalston. They were sleeping on the floor of the village hall – with two non-commissioned officers sleeping in one ante-room, and Lieutenant Hills, a First World War veteran, sleeping in the other – when the siren went off. Mr Hills, who had spent the evening in the local pub and hadn't wasted the time, raced down the hall in his pyjamas shouting, 'Fritz is overhead, Fritz is overhead! And what have I got, what *have* I got?

One revolver, two rifles and fifty bloody fools!' One couldn't help but sympathise!

Iain didn't particularly mind the work, which was usually loading and unloading trucks, especially when it was in the fresh air. But the meaninglessness of it all was brought home rather forcibly at Carlisle, where half of them were loading Carr's biscuits on to trains for Glasgow, while the other half unloaded biscuits made by Wyllie, Barr and Ross in Glasgow.

Many of the non-commissioned officers were quite decent men who found themselves in the Pioneer Corps because of some physical disability. They resented the injustice of the stigma attached to the Pioneers, who were regarded as almost sub-human by some of the other regiments, and thus felt sorry for the NCC who were even lower down the scale than they were. There were others, however, who used their little power to make life as difficult as possible, and yet others who found the conchies incomprehensible.

Clearly, a lot of talent was being wasted, but they soon learned not to ask for a transfer to the Medical Corps, the Pay Corps or the Educational Corps, where one would have thought their training could have been put to better use. To do that they had to renounce their conscientious objections and as soon as anyone did that they were whipped away to an Infantry Regiment. (In fairness, it must be said that they were not the only men who would have preferred not to be involved in the fighting. If it had been possible to choose, those regiments would have been oversubscribed. The COs had to be seen to be paying a price for the stand they were taking.)

A few from another company were allowed to join the Parachute Medical Corps without first agreeing to carry weapons, but they were all shot down before they reached the ground and the experiment was not repeated.

Dave Waddell wanted to join the Friends' Ambulance Unit. First, he had to refuse orders. Then, if he was sentenced to three months in gaol, he was entitled to another tribunal and could ask to be sent to the FAU. He was sentenced to one day short of the qualifying period and had a very hard time of it in Durham Gaol. When he came out he refused again, served the same sentence, and returned to Carlisle apparently a broken man.

He had been the fittest man in the camp, but now he could barely walk, had lost a lot of weight and had aged ten years. He refused again. At this point Major Standford decided that enough was enough and spoke to the Medical Officer, who had him invalided out. He returned home to Glasgow, where his fiancée, Anna, helped to nurse him back to health. He then joined the Friends' Relief Service in time to be involved in the humanitarian work following the liberation of Holland.

Iain was still interested in Friends, and one day Dennis Carey said, 'At church parade on Sunday I'm going to ask to go to a Friends' Meeting. Will you come with me?'

'Well, I usually go to the Scots Kirk, but only because we have to go somewhere and I like to hear the Scots voices,' he replied, 'So, yes – I'll come. At least we'll get a bit of peace!'

On the Sunday morning, they lined up as usual and the sergeant started the familiar litany.

'OBs fall-out! EBs fallout! C of E fall-out! Romans fall out! Methodists...' and so on through all the denominations, until only Dennis and Iain were left standing.

'And what demolition [sic] are you?' he demanded.

With a straight face Dennis replied, 'We're Friends, sergeant.'

'Dammit, man – I know you're friends,' he stormed, 'But what church do you go to?'

Dennis explained that the right name for the Quakers was 'The Religious Society of Friends' and they were allowed to go. Iain enjoyed the meeting and decided he would probably repeat the experiment when the war was over. (He did, in fact, join the Society several years after the war.)

Before that, however, against the advice of all his friends, he had volunteered to be used as a guinea pig in experiments to find a treatment for mustard gas. Of all the horrors of the First War that he had heard of or read about, mustard gas attacks seemed far the most horrendous. If he could help anyone faced with that he felt he should. So off he went to the establishment now known as Porton Down. There, mustard gas was dropped on to his arm and an American ointment was applied. Unfortunately, that particular ointment was of no use at all. He developed huge blisters on his arm and on his neck, part of his arm turned green and the pain under his armpit was indescribable. The medics diagnosed septicaemia, and this being before the advent of antibiotics, amputation seemed inevitable. By some miracle, his system fought back and he kept his arm, but it was a very sick man who was sent back to his unit, excused duties until the horrible sore on his arm healed up.

This took a long time. His friends moved out to Penrith and he was left with a hut full of Plymouth Brethren, with whom he had nothing in common. He mooned around the camp with his arm in a sling, talking to anyone who would talk to him. However, the minute the doctor gave permission, the sergeant-major said, 'I think you'd better go out to Longtown. Summer's coming and a nice job in the fresh air will build you up!' They were digging the foundations for a new camp.

At least some of his friends were at Longtown, so he set off with relief, and it was there that I first met him, when I was working as a volunteer in the Methodist canteen, in the spring of 1942. He still looked a sick man to me, but it was someone else who told me what was wrong with him. He never mentioned it and I have just heard the details for the first time after fifty years of marriage.

From Longtown he returned to Carlisle, and from there to the frightful conditions in Lancaster. That didn't do him a lot of good and he developed chronic sinusitis, for which he had to have a major operation soon after he returned to civilian life, and a stomach condition which the MO described as a 'nervous stomach'. However, he soldiered on. There wasn't much option. His detachment continued to be moved from one place to another. They were in Preston for a while, then in Failsworth near Manchester.

From Failsworth he managed to arrange a swap with someone in Carlisle whose wife lived in Warrington, and so we were together again for a while. Life in camp had become even more unnecessarily restrictive under a new sergeant who hated the conchies. They each had their own way of coping with this. Iain's was so bizarre that he got the reputation of being not quite right in the head.

He found that the army simply couldn't cope with the unexpected. So he owned up to things he couldn't possibly have done: 'It was me, sergeant. I did it. Put me on a charge,' he would beg. Anyone with a grain of sense would have taken him at his word and soon put a stop to that, but the sergeant suspected that he was being 'got at' and refused to play. 'Get lost, soldier!' he would growl, and then confide to the sergeant-major, 'That chap is going to keep on owning up to things that we know he had nothing to do with, knowing that no-one will believe him. Then he'll do something terrible like setting the camp on fire – and own up to that and get off with it!

(All this was reported with glee by the mess orderly).

Their leave had been messed about with till nobody knew what they were doing. They would be all set to go and their leave would be cancelled at the last minute for no reason other than to show who was boss. Not invariably, but often enough to leave everyone unsettled. The point that was being made was that all leave was a *privilege* and not a right, but there was no need to rub it in in this fashion.

Iain turned this on its head. When his leave was due, his pass was all made out, but he didn't go. The sergeant went into the office hoping to catch him trying to get his pass early so that he could slope off to catch the Glasgow train, but he never turned up – not even at the proper time. The next day he managed to get down to the sheds where they were working without being seen leaving camp. The sergeant was convinced that he had gone AWOL and a hue and cry was set up.

When he marched into camp with the others that night, the sergeant was dumbfounded, 'Where the hell have you been?' he thundered.

'Working in the sheds, sergeant,' replied Iain, innocence shining from his face.

'But you're supposed to be on leave!'

'Yes, sergeant, but I didn't know I *had* to go. I'll go tomorrow, if you like,' offered this model soldier. The detachment held its breath, but the sergeant admitted defeat.

'You'll catch the train to Glasgow tonight – and that's an order!' he said. Since that was what he had intended to do in the first place, Iain was quite happy. There wasn't much point in going on leave on Saturday as he would be stranded in Glasgow, there being no trains to Oban on a Sunday, and he'd spent Saturday evening with me!

There were many incidents like this and he always got away with it. He hadn't done anything that was exactly wrong, and it was so easy to wrong-foot bullies of that kind. All great fun in a way, and a great waste in another, and it did his health no good at all. By this time there was very little that he could eat without vomiting and, in the end, he was sent to a very sympathetic Jewish medical officer.

'I seem to be dealing with Britain's oppressed minorities this morning,' he smiled. 'Two Welshmen and now a Scot. And what's wrong with you? It's very clear that something is.'

Iain told him his story, the MO examined his record, and then gave him a thorough medical examination. 'You are not going to get any better until you get out of the army,' the doctor told him. 'I'm going to give you a medical discharge.'

'Oh, don't do that,' Iain pleaded, 'I'm not working my ticket. I've stuck it so far and it can't be that long now. I'll stick it out!'

'Well it's up to you, but this isn't doing anyone any good,' was the reply. Iain settled for a bottle of useless medicine and his comrades decided that they now had proof positive that he was mad!

The war in Europe ended in May 1945, and we became engaged a fortnight later. In the September of that year, he was moved to Bicester, where they were employed laying tracks for a light railway. They were there when the war with Japan ended, and Major Clark, a Scot whom they all admired, decided that as far as possible the time spent waiting for demobilisation would be devoted to educational pursuits. They set up a repertory group, which Iain joined, and toured various centres playing *Twelfth Night* and Vanbrugh's *The Confederacy* . By this time I had found a post as a dispenser in Petts Wood and we were able to meet at week-ends. In April 1946, he was moved to Taunton, and shortly afterwards he was demobbed.

7

Lochgilphead – Amalgamation

After years of dreaming of his demob the event, when it finally came, proved to be an anti-climax. His service ended officially at midnight on 30th April 1946, and a group of men who were leaving at the same time were bussed out of the camp at one minute past midnight, while the rest of the camp was asleep. They were dumped on the station at Taunton to catch a train to Bristol where, after hanging about for a considerable time, they boarded a train for Leeds. Some of them dozed intermittently, but they were afraid that if they all slept they would miss their stop, and most got very little sleep. From Leeds it was a comparatively short distance to York, where an army truck conveyed them to the barracks. It was not yet nine thirty in the morning.

In the barracks they were processed through the demobilisation routine, given a civilian identity card, a suit, overcoat, shoes and a felt hat, the twin of the one he had so hated in Oban! He then made his way back to the station to catch the next train to Edinburgh. He had had so many plans for the first night of his final leave but in the event he was so tired that, still wearing his uniform, he made his way to the YMCA hostel. He fixed up a bed for the night and somehow found himself in a church at the west end of Princes Street saying an unspecified and unformulated, but deeply felt, 'Thank-you.' Then he found something to eat and went to bed.

The next day, now wearing his new civilian outfit, he went to see Mrs Gilbert to pick up his things, which she had kept for him all these years, and then went to the office at Leith. Mr Gorrie was delighted to see him, as indeed he had been whenever Iain had looked in to withdraw a little more from his account during the war years. It was pretty threadbare by this time. Neither Mr Gorrie nor Miss Thorburn had ever failed to send him a card at Christmas. Even more surprisingly, Mr Hall, the formidable manager of Edinburgh Head Office, had sent him a little note and a parcel of magazines each year!

However, the decision as to his future did not lie in their hands, so he caught the train to Glasgow and made his way to Glasgow Head Office. Mr Cunningham welcomed him, rather more formally, since they had not met before. He gave his official permission for our marriage and told Iain that there was a job for him at Lochgilphead if he wanted it, but he would have to start on the first of June.

That gave him four weeks to arrange our wedding, get married, have a honeymoon and find somewhere for us to live. I could be no help, as I was in Petts Wood and would have to work my notice before I could go home. He did manage a week or so winding down a little in Oban, but when he went to see the Registrar in Longtown he was told that one of us would have to be resident in Longtown for two weeks before the wedding. So he spent the next two weeks with my parents, arranging the wedding and cutting sticks! My mother had only one cure for nerves, which she later passed on to Iain as a hint on how to deal with me in moments of stress: 'Give her something to do with her hands. It never fails!' Now she applied this medicine to him, and he must have chopped enough sticks to last them the winter!

Iain had to get permission from my father as I was under twenty-one, and he was rather flattered when the registrar added, 'And what about *your* father's permission?' He was thirty-one at the time! His father had died two years before, but his mother and his uncle John, from Stirling, were able to attend the wedding and his cousin, 'young John', agreed to be the best man. As I got home only the day before, our wedding was a low-key affair, pretty well confined to family. However, we were able to spend a week in Ayr before taking the steamer from Gourock to Ardrishaig.

Things were difficult at first. The rooms Iain had been promised were no longer available, but with Cewan's help we found a single room in a flat on the ground floor of the tenement Iain had lived in before the war. The first of June was a local holiday, so he had to work for only a few hours on that first morning. He was given a handbook that had been prepared for returning ex-servicemen explaining any changes in the bank's procedures that had taken place during their absence. Yet both Lochgilphead and the office seemed to have changed very little. The buildings were noticeably shabbier, but otherwise the war seemed to have passed them by.

Mr Munro was still the manager, but Donald Cormack had been moved to Edinburgh and John Pollock, an older man, had taken his place. John hated the place and wanted out of it. He, too, had found difficulty in finding somewhere to live and was staying in the Argyll Hotel. Iain commented,

'I don't think he's really trying. He wants to use the fact that he can't find a place to stay as an excuse to get away as soon as possible.'

Miss MacVicar (Barbara) had taken charge of the ledgers, and Mr Munro made it clear that although she had not passed any exams and was junior to Iain, that was how it was going to stay. That was fair enough, as she had been doing the job for some time, but acting as an all-purpose clerk alongside Jean Gillies, the junior, was a come-down from the busy ledger desk at Leith.

Ardrishaig had once again been made into a separate office and his friend Ian Bulloch, who like most of his contemporaries in the bank had been a commissioned officer, was appointed as manager. It couldn't have happened to a nicer fellow, and they remained good friends, but it emphasised Iain's position. Although he had finished his English examinations while he was in Carlisle, it was clear that it was going to be a long time before they would be of any use to him. He would have liked to go as second man in Ardrishaig as he could have worked happily alongside Ian, but that was out of the question as the post was already held by Mr Munro's daughter, Amy.

Much later, he told me, 'If I hadn't been married I would have got out then and gone over to the West of Eire and found myself a job as a 'boots' in some small country hotel.' His self-esteem had reached an all-time low, and the difficulty we were having in finding somewhere decent to live didn't help.

The business had changed very little, though the work of the Forestry Commission had increased enormously and the regimented forests of Sitka Spruce were spreading over more and more hillsides. Environmentalists and those who wanted to preserve the barren beauty of the landscape hated them, but they provided work for many and the foresters themselves were a cheerful bunch of men. Iain enjoyed Thursday mornings when they all came in around the same time to collect cash to pay the wages and the office buzzed with their banter.

In Argyll, the county offices and the police still provided much of the business. The farmers were more prosperous than they had been before the war, but on the whole the farms were small and most of the farmers were far from wealthy. The tourist trade was picking up very slowly, rationing was still in place, and most people still used public transport.

The accountants, who were all single men, didn't stay long. Johnny Pollock was succeeded by Wilson MacKenzie, and he, in turn, was succeeded by Jack Burt who didn't get on with Mr Munro and was relieved to get away after a few months. Around the time Robert Marlborough took over, Iain was appointed as teller. 'I loved that job as I always liked dealing with people,' he said. Since by that time we had moved into a furnished house on the Manse Brae, and I had found part-time work as a dispenser at the Argyll and Bute hospital, things were looking up and we were feeling more settled.

The customers provided an endless source of interest and entertainment. Iain loves to tell about Calum Iain, a nurse at the hospital: 'He had saved earnestly to buy a new car. It was his pride and joy and he spent hours admiring it and polishing it.' One filthy wet day in the middle of winter when the tide was high and the wind was throwing water at the windows of the bank (whether it was rain or sea was impossible to tell) and it was almost impossible to hold one's feet on the front street, Calum Iain came in shrouded in waterproofs and well-nigh exhausted.

'Where's the car today, Calum?' Iain asked, 'You must be soaked!' The Argyll and Bute was more than a mile out of town.

'I left it in the garage,' he said. 'It would have got filthy in this weather. So I just used the bike.'

Mr Munro was an accomplished amateur conjuror. Iain went into the office on one occasion to find him teasing one of his simpler farming customers.

'What's that in your ear, Donald?' he asked, as he took a shilling from it. Then as the astonished Donald rubbed his ear in complete mystification, he went on, 'There's one in the other. You really should look after your money,' and he added another coin to the first. Iain exited rapidly, feeling that this was not the moment to interrupt.

Mr Munro was one of the bank's characters and he evoked an odd mixture of exasperation and affection in his staff. He really cared about his customers and took endless trouble to help them if he could. Mr Mackenzie remarked one day, 'It seems to me that when you are dying in this place, if you are a Catholic you send for the priest, and if you are a Protestant you send for Jimmy Munro!' And there was much truth in it. He helped many families in time of crisis. People thought nothing of sending for him to some remote farmhouse where he would sit with the relatives through the night as their loved one lay dying. Frequently he was sent for to make a will, a service for which he never charged, but perhaps the most unlikely, but perfectly true, story was of the night when he was cut off by floods and had to be rescued by Amy and her uncle after he'd gone out late at night to insure a newly born foal.

Dedication such as this endeared him to the customers and it certainly paid off in the growth of the business, though I am not convinced that was the only reason he did it as he really enjoyed helping people – but he could be exasperating to work with as the accountant was never right!

Mr Munro also had an eagle eye for mistakes. He would look over the shoulder of someone working and say, 'That's not right – there's a something. I don't know what it is but there's a something.' He was almost always right. It was a sort of sixth sense that comes with long experience. Yet it was maddening that when the staff had been checking and re-checking to find an elusive discrepancy, he could stroll out of his room and put his finger on it almost at once. Frequently after a long search for a small amount the missing coin would be found in the turn-up of the teller's trousers!

Mr Munro had no time for Head Office. 'What do those idiots sitting on high stools in Glasgow know about country banking?' he would growl and on one occasion when Head Office came on the phone asking for him, Iain found him up a tree in the garden cutting off a diseased branch. 'Tell them I'm busily engaged in administrative duties,' he said loftily, 'I'll call them back later.'

Certainly, the inspectors were baffled by some of the things they found in the branch. 'This is the same writing,' they said, looking at two cheques. 'Either the man is signing his wife's cheques, or she is signing his.'

'Yes, that's right,' said Mr Munro, quite unworried, 'she signs for her sons too. She does the banking for the whole family. They live at the back of beyond and never leave the farm. I go out and see them from time to time and it's all above board; they're quite happy to leave it to her.'

'Yes, well it won't do,' said the inspector. 'You'll need to get proper signatures from them all.' But nothing was done about it and it was a different pair of inspectors the next time and they didn't pick it up.

Another family all signed their name differently. To illustrate the point I will call them MacNeil: it was a similar name. Between them they managed MacNeil, MacNeill, McNeil, Macneil and Mcneil. Nor were they consistent – they just used whichever version occurred to them at the time. In such circumstances it was very important to know your customer. A signature by itself told you very little.

Mc and Mac could make for much confusion. The Milk Board made out one cheque wrongly so that Mr Mc was £1000 over, and Mr Mac was £1000 short. Neither paid much attention to money paid into their accounts and it was the bank that noticed the mistake and had the correction made.

'Have a look at this!' said Barbara. 'Donnie Mc never had a milk cheque that size in his life. Don't tell me he's bought a whole new herd!'

'No,' said Iain, 'it will be Donnie Mac's. Have a look at his cheque.' But if they hadn't known the size of their customers' herds they wouldn't have spotted the discrepancy. Mr Munro's jaunts up country were not without purpose.

After a few years in Lochgilphead, Iain was sent to take charge at Tarbert as the manager was ill and Gordon Audsley, the older of the two junior members of staff, was still quite young. Mr Couper had moved on and his place had been taken by Mr Campbell, who always wore full Highland dress, as his previous branch had been Braemar, and he thought of himself as 'the Queen's Banker'. It is to be hoped that he did not get his ideas of economy from the company he claimed to have kept, for to say he was careful was the greatest of understatements.

It was mid-winter when Iain arrived and the office was cold, so around ten o'clock he threw the shovelful of coal beside the fireplace on to the fire. Gordon was horrified. 'That's our ration for the day!' he said.

'You're kidding,' Iain said. 'That won't last till lunchtime. Away out to the coal cellar and get some more. If Mr Campbell is as ill as he's supposed to be he'll be none the wiser.'

'He keeps the key in the house, and you won't get it from Mrs Campbell either,' retorted Gordon. 'I tell you, you've done it now.'

'But doesn't the bank pay for his heat and light?' asked Iain, still not entirely convinced. 'They pay for Mr Munro's.'

'Of course they do but it makes no difference. Even in the house they sit with rugs over their knees to save fuel.' By lunchtime the fire was nearly out, and they raced round to Casci's tearoom for a hot drink and a heat. They balanced with frozen fingers and Iain went back to Casci's to wait for the bus home. It was the most uncomfortable three weeks he ever spent in the bank.

However, while he was there he saw a notice about a new Diploma in Trustee and Executry and noted, especially, that a cash prize was being offered to those members who obtained it. It wasn't much and few took up the challenge, but our financial state being what it was, Iain felt it was too good to miss. He began studying as soon as he returned from Tarbert, but he insisted that we couldn't afford a correspondence course so he worked on his own from text books provided by the county librarian, Mr Reid. It wasn't ideal, as often the books didn't have the most up-to-date information, but the bank gave him a fortnight's intensive experience in the Trustee and Executry department which was invaluable and, after three years hard study, he finally made it.

The course included a paper on investment which seems to have been of great practical value to his customers, judging by comments some of them have made to me, but he never speculated himself. I don't think he was ever sure about the morality of the market! His knowledge of executry came in handy when the time came for him to retire, as will be seen in the final chapter.

Jean Gillies left to get married and was replaced by Thelma Stewart, who took over the cash when Mr Marlborough's successor, Dave Callum, moved on and Iain was promoted to accountant. A series of apprentices were engaged, the first being Hamish McKinnon, who had just finished his two years National Service. He was a great favourite with our children and many years later became manager at Campbeltown. By that time our grown-up daughter was working as a clinical psychologist in Sheffield, though she still kept her account in Campbeltown. Her handbag had been stolen and she had notified the bank. The secretary called her and announced in a voice dripping with innuendo and curiosity, 'There's a man asking for you, Jane. He has a gorgeous Scotch [sic] voice, but when I asked for his name he said, "Just tell her it's Hamish."'

Jane returned from the phone and announced, 'That was my bank manager!'

'Pull the other one,' said the girl. 'Bank managers don't announce themselves as Hamish!'

'They do where I come from,' was the cool reply.

Hamish was followed by Alec, a bright boy who was born street-wise, but who had a lot to learn about diplomacy when he first entered the bank. The inspectors arrived and Mr Munro told Alec to take them in a cup of coffee. He did as he was bid and asked, 'Does either o' you tak sugar?' When they indicated that they both did, he banged down a bottle of saccharin tablets and left them to it. Iain wondered what Mr Robb would have said to that!

At that time they were frequently interrupted by a little old lady, who had been a good customer but was now decidedly odd, and had taken to wearing two hats, one on top of the other. She really was the bane of Mr Munro's life, as she thought he could solve all her problems. One day a large, rather formidable lady with the same name came into the office and asked to speak to the manager. Ever helpful, Alec opened the door of Mr Munro's room and announced, 'There's a Mrs Fletcher to see you.'

'Is it the funny woman?' mouthed Mr Munro.

'Yes,' replied Alec.

'Then tell her to come back tomorrow, I'm busy,' was the reply, and Alec dutifully relayed the message.

Later Iain asked, 'Why didn't you want to see the vet's wife? She was quite put out!'

'But I didn't,' began the mystified manager – and then the penny dropped. He swung round to Alec.

'You said it was the funny woman,' he charged.

'Well, she looked funny to me,' said the irrepressible apprentice.

Mr Munro raced to get the car out, but as Iain said much later, 'Dear only knows how he talked himself out of that one, but he did!'

Iain was the accountant when the Bank of Scotland took over the Union Bank. The run up to this event, which occurred in 1955, involved a tremendous amount of extra work as nearly all the bank's procedures had to be changed. Mr Munro was due to retire in 1955 so, not entirely unreasonably, he refused to have anything to do with it. Fortunately, by that time we had our own house not far from the bank, so Iain was able to dash home for a meal in the evening before returning to work.

He found Mr Munro's 'I don't want to know' attitude hard to bear at times and on onc occasion he arrived home in a state of fury that was so unlike him that I was really worried. He went back to work and at about eleven o'clock I went to bed. At midnight I got up again and as one o'clock approached I went round to the bank to find it in total darkness. 'Where on earth is he?' I wondered. I walked round the block but at that time of night the village was completely deserted. I went back to the house and waited a little longer with my imagination working overtime. Should I go to the police station and get them to search the canal? Mrs Munro and Amy were away. Even in that mood he couldn't have murdered the boss – could he? 'Don't be ridiculous,' I told myself. 'The very worst that can have happened is that he's told Mr Munro to keep his job, and now he's wandering around somewhere wondering how to tell me!'

I walked slowly back to the bank house and met him emerging from the back gate. He had obviously been drinking and was now a friend to all the world!

'What on earth have you been doing? Have you any idea what time it is? I have been worried sick!' I stormed. 'I had begun to think you'd killed him and drowned yourself, the mood you were in.'

'No, no, no, no, poor old man,' he said. 'I took in the keys about half-past eleven and, right enough, I was mad at him. But he was lonely, and he said "Have a drink and cheer me up," and we got yarning about the old days. You know how it is?'

Indeed I did, so I just said, 'Well it's now two o'clock and I wouldn't like the head you are going to have in the morning. So for heaven's sake come to bed!'

In fact, this incident shows just how much stress the two men were under at the time. Mr Munro was practically a teetotaller, but he wasn't well and his wife was undergoing major surgery in one of the Glasgow hospitals. He was facing retirement, the upheaval of finding a new house, the thought of coping with the removal with an invalid wife, and concern for Amy on whom most of the work must fall. She, like Iain, was probably working overtime coping with the changeover at Ardrishaig as well as running between her mother in Glasgow and her father at home. All this must, at that moment, have seemed just too much. Certainly, drinking with a member of staff was totally out of character.

Iain wasn't a drinker, either, but the extra work of dealing with the changeover without much support from Mr Munro had brought him close to the end of his tether so with hindsight this incident seems to have diffused a fraught situation in a happily harmless fashion.

Somehow or other the transfer to the Bank of Scotland was made and shortly afterwards Mr Munro retired. The staff made a presentation, but though I'm sure the customers would have wanted to do something to mark the occasion, the opportunity was spoilt because one of them asked Mr Munro himself for a list of names. Obviously, he refused and said he didn't want anything and the staff knew nothing about this at the time. The sensible thing would have been to ask the accountant or put a notice in the local paper, or even on the local grapevine. People just needed to know who to give their donations to. It was all a great pity and an unsuitable end to a long and devoted career. He moved to a villa on the Manse Brae and lived for many contented years in retirement. When he died, many years later, it was Dochie MacDougall who wrote a most moving obituary in the local paper.

8
Lochgilphead – Under New Management

'Upright' is the one word which, above all others, springs to mind to describe Tom Sim, the new manager at Lochgilphead. He was a big man, tall and broad-shouldered but with no tendency to run to fat – the miles he walked with his wife every week-end saw to that! Meeting him for the first time one might have imagined him to be a high-ranking policeman or, since he came from the north-east, have seen in his ruddy colour and sandy hair signs of Viking descent. A formidable man, a fair man, a transparently honest man, but not one to be messed about.

At first, the staff were wary and the customers were intimidated. The easy going atmosphere seemed to have departed forever. Mr Sim's diction didn't help either, as he spoke with grammatical precision and never used a short word if a long one would do. And yet, he had a very pleasant wife, a gentle good-looking woman, a 'lady' – the good Scots word 'perjink' springs to mind, and visions of Edinburgh matrons drinking tea – but kind and approachable. He had two sons with whom he was obviously on excellent terms. We saw little of the older boy who was working in Alva, where Mr Sim had previously been the manager, but the younger boy spent a couple of terms in the local school before being sent to finish his secondary education at Dollar Academy. He was a good mixer and well-behaved but he wasn't at all scared of his father, though he showed the easy, friendly respect that Iain would have expected from David when he was older, but no more.

We began to suspect that the private man might be rather less intimidating than he appeared to be in public. Gradually, as he assured himself that things were not slack in the office and that the staff *were* giving of their best, he seemed to unbend slightly. The customers who needed his help found it was forthcoming and that his advice was sound, but, though he would visit customers at their request if a formal appointment had been made, he never just 'went missing' as Mr Munro had done.

From Iain's point of view, it was wonderful to have a manager who was there when he was needed and who was entirely predictable. If a customer complained, the boss did not immediately attack the member of staff involved. He investigated; and if he thought the staff member was in the right, he said so and explained why. Of course, if they were in the wrong they could expect to hear about it – Mr Sim didn't mince his words – but once they got used to the new regime they liked it. They worked hard but knew that their efforts were respected.

One day Iain came home and told me, 'Mrs Sim and Ian are going away for a week or so. We'll have to have the boss in for a meal.'

I was horrified. By this time I was used to cooking for an extended family, but we had never gone in for formal entertaining and I was sure Mr Sim would expect things to be done properly. Moreover, we had married when the shortages were greatest and we had not started life with full canteens of cutlery and the beautiful dinner services and napery that Iain's contemporaries who had married just before the war could boast. We had a collection of bits and pieces spared by our families and our china had been acquired at auction sales, piecemeal. I did try to set the table nicely, even for family meals, but I was still smarting from the occasion when the two-year old David had looked at his dinner plate and side plate and exclaimed triumphantly, 'Look, Mummy – I got a match!'

No matter, it had to be done and at least the children could be relied on to behave properly at meal-times, so an evening was set. It proved to be a revelation. Mr Sim on duty and Tom Sim off duty were two entirely different people. The slightly pompous formal language was discarded and as he relaxed into his native Buchan dialect, it became clear to me that at work Mr Sim was speaking in what was to him a foreign language, hence the painful correctness. I know now that people in the north-east have virtually two languages, the one they use to each other – which is incomprehensible to an outsider – and the one they use in more formal situations and when speaking to strangers. This was the first time I had seen this in action, though, of course, he moderated the Doric for our benefit.

He had been brought up in the fishing port of Fraserburgh and was full of stories of worthies on and off the boats. It became clear that he had worked hard through night school and correspondence courses to further his own education, but he had also become involved in amateur drama, and when two people with experience in that field get together the stories flow fast and furious.

In the end, as might have been predicted, they got round to stories about the bank. Iain had some odd stories to tell but Mr Sim could cap them all. We sat round the dining room fire after the children went to bed and we laughed until it hurt. His story of the manager in one country branch who was drinking too much is vivid still.

'The inspectors arrived at the front door and we pushed him out at the back and locked him in the coal cellar. Then we told the inspectors that he was away up country at a funeral and wouldn't be back until late!' This was *Mr Sim* talking. I couldn't believe it, but it was one of the happiest evenings I have ever spent.

Next morning, of course, normal relations prevailed, but I suspect that Mr Sim had moved very close to Mr Couper in Iain's private hierarchy. They worked well together, but that didn't prevent the manager from saying, before he left Iain in charge of the bank while he was on holiday, 'If any problems turn up, don't do what you think is right. Do what you think I would do in the circumstances. When you get your own office, you can do it your way. This is my office – so do it my way.'

But it was said with great good humour and Iain answered comfortably, 'Fair enough. I've a good idea what you would do in most circumstances and I'm quite happy with that.' Mr Munro would not have been so blunt, but Iain would have felt that whatever he did might be wrong.

The staff were beginning to relax and the new junior, Mary Gillies, a bright, hardworking youngster was quite a favourite with the boss. Her mother worked in the local laundry where she collected all the local gossip. Mary would come in in the morning bursting with the latest tit-bit and say, 'C'm here, c'm here – have you heard this?' and would gather them round her so that she could pass on her news. She had a good stage whisper, and Mr Sim had acute hearing, so frequently her story would be followed by a low rumble of laughter from the manager's office and she would colour up and mutter, 'Oh, Lord – he wasn't meant to hear that.'

He heard a lot more than people realised.

Mr Sim was already an elder in the Church of Scotland before he came to Lochgilphead, and in that church, ordination as an elder is for life. He quickly took his place in the local congregation and soon became session clerk. In that role he was responsible for the arrangements when a new minister was to be inducted and it goes without saying that those arrangements had been planned with the meticulous efficiency appropriate to a royal wedding. Yet even the best planner would be unlikely to allow for the possibility that a young minister would become seriously ill on the morning of his ordination, as happened then.

Mr Sim received the news with stoic calm – he knew all the correct procedures. To Iain he said, 'You will have to take charge for half an hour or so. I must go and adhibit the proper notice to the board outside the church.'

As soon as he was outside the office Mary burst out, 'Why can he no juist stick it up like onybody else!'

Mary was a great favourite and the staff were looking forward to her wedding, to which they were all invited. Like many Scottish weddings, it was to be held in the late afternoon, in this case in Ardrishaig Church, and was to be followed by a dinner and dance in a local hotel. They had all their regular customers primed not to bring in any large lodgements or anything complicated that day, so that the girls could get away to the wedding as soon as the doors closed and the men could do a quick balance and get to the reception, at least. Then the inspectors arrived.

Fortunately that pair were understanding and didn't put any unnecessary blocks in their way. Coming in after lunch one of them asked Iain, 'What's on today? Why are all the flags flying?'

'Mary Gillies is getting married,' he said.

'Oh, come on. You've made that point already, and we've said we won't hold you up, but all the flags are flying down at the green. There must be something special going on.'

'I've told you – Mary's getting married – and Mary's special,' teased Iain and would say no more. Actually it was quite true, the flags had been put up for Mary's wedding. The flags went up for every wedding, provided the father of the bride paid the Town Council a pound for the workman to put them up. It was one of the nicer things about living in a small burgh.

By this time, apart from Gordon Graham in Inveraray, Iain was the senior man in the district. Given the small staff at Inveraray, Gordon could never be spared so Iain was frequently called on at very short notice to deputise for managers who had taken ill, or were on courses or on holiday. They were not all as specific as Mr Sim in their instructions. He arrived off the bus at Inveraray to be told by Mr Beaumont, 'Gordon's in hospital, I've got 'flu and I feel like death. I'm off to bed – the girls will keep you right!'

In Ardrishaig, on another occasion, he didn't have even that much guidance. He arrived to take charge of the office single handed, and couldn't find where Ian kept his back-up supplies of pay-in slips. He searched frantically through drawers and cupboards while an irate customer wondered aloud, 'What on earth kin' o' a bank is this? They canna even gie ye a pay-in slip when ye ask fur a yin!'

After the take-over by the Bank of Scotland the question of relief became even more fraught. The new Head Office was in Edinburgh and the people there seemed to have no conception of the geography of the West of Scotland. For the benefit of readers who are in the same state of ignorance I should explain that the west coast, like Norway, is broken up by deep indentations – fiords in Norway, sea-lochs in Scotland. This means that so far as public transport is concerned, the land is broken into large areas all with direct links to Glasgow, but totally unconnected to each other for all practical purposes. (For at least twenty years after the war the banks and other public bodies assumed their staffs would travel by public transport.) For many years, for example, Argyll County Council met in Glasgow because it was the only place that all the councillors could get to easily, or relatively easily. Head Office seemed to look at a map and measure distance as the crow flies.

Relieving in Inveraray, Iain was needed back in Lochgilphead – urgently. He phoned Edinburgh and suggested that someone be sent to replace him from Alexandria or Helensburgh, both about forty miles away, and both easily accessible by bus. 'Rubbish,' he was told. 'They are not even in the same county! We will send Mr McKinnon from Campbeltown.' So Hamish caught the 9am bus to Ardrishaig, took time out to have lunch with his mother, caught the earliest possible bus from Lochgilphead to Inveraray and arrived after the office was closed for the day. The boy from Alexandria would have been there before lunch in which case Iain could have been back in Lochgilphead by one o'clock. Mr Sim was furious.

So was Ian Bulloch the day his boy was posted to Kyle of Lochalsh. He asked for relief, as the journey would take two days: one to get to Glasgow and one to get from Glasgow to Kyle of Lochalsh. They wouldn't hear of it. 'What is to stop him from going via Oban?' they asked.

'The fact that when he gets to Oban, he'll still have to take the train to Glasgow to get to Kyle of Lochalsh!' he stormed, but it did him no good. They just didn't believe him. Everyone who served in the bank at that time has a fund of similar stories. It must be easier now that most young people have cars, but the distances are still great and you still travel north from Campbeltown for over seventy miles to Inveraray before going south again towards Glasgow, yet it is no great distance as the crow flies.

Stewart, Balfour and Sutherland, a firm of Campbeltown lawyers, maintained an office above the Bank of Scotland at Lochgilphead and each Wednesday a junior partner would travel up to see clients in Tarbert and Mid-Argyll. When Iain first went there A.I.B. Stewart was a regular visitor but by this time David Fairbairn usually made the run. One of the bank staff at the time also came from Campbeltown, and, like many Campbeltonians, couldn't get back often enough. He went home every week-end, returning by bus on Monday mornings just in time for the nine o'clock opening.

One week that winter was unusually snowy and Mr Sim had warned him not to go home at the week-end if there was any danger that he would not get back in time, but as it happened the week-end was clear and he made it safely. However, he pushed his luck a little too far. There was something special on in Campbeltown on the Wednesday night and, although there were some flakes of snow floating around, he reckoned he could take a lift home with David Fairbairn, go to the show and get the bus back in the morning. In the morning the bus stuck at Glenbarr. The boy made a tremendous effort to get to the phone to explain what had happened, but Mr Sim was not to be placated. 'I have a rod in pickle for that young man,' he told Iain, 'Make sure he reports to me the minute he gets in.' Iain passed on the message, verbatim.

'But what does it mean?' asked the penitent.

'I reckon you are about to find out!' replied the hard-hearted accountant – but the boy survived, albeit somewhat chastened.

The hardest stint of relief Iain ever had to undertake was in Dunoon at the time of the Greenock Fair holidays. Glasgow and its surrounding towns take holidays at 'the Fair'. Glasgow or Greenock or Paisley Fair Fortnight is the equivalent of a Lancashire Wakes Week – a time when all the big manufacturers close down and everyone goes on holiday. Iain gave up taking an English newspaper in disgust the day he read in *The Observer* that the A74 had been packed with people *going to* the Glasgow Fair. That road had certainly been crowded – but the crowds were of people streaming out of Glasgow not into it!

Dunoon was always busy with summer visitors during the Fair

weeks, but at that time the Americans had newly taken over the Holy Loch and the place was already packed with American sailors. The manager there had more than enough to do at the best of times but, when Iain got the SOS to go and help out, he was working with three senior staff short: one was on holiday and two were ill. All he had in the way of staff was a junior clerk borrowed from Glasgow, an apprentice and 'a wee girl'! Clearly the matter was urgent, so Iain caught the next boat and, though the office was closed by the time he arrived, he went in and started work immediately.

He stayed in the Craigen Hotel across the road from the bank and the next morning even as he and the young clerk were eating their breakfasts they could see that the manager was already at work opening the mail. 'It was frantic,' Iain told me afterwards. 'The young chap from Glasgow acted as first teller, I was accountant and second teller. The wee girl spread his notes and the manager spread mine – we certainly had no time to do it as we were going flat out as long as the bank was open.'

'What exactly does spreading notes entail?' I ventured to ask. He looked at me in total astonishment. Could I have been married to him for all those years without knowing something as basic as that? Well, yes I could, quite easily. A banker's wife doesn't have the run of the bank the way a shopkeeper's wife does a shop. I probably knew as little about the details of my husband's work as anyone married into the secret service – confidentiality was absolute. So I asked again.

'Well really it's a matter of sorting them out,' he said. I'd guessed that much so I waited for more. 'At Dunoon there was a wooden box on each of the two window-sills behind the counter,' he explained carefully, as to a very stupid child.

'Each had nine pigeon holes – one for each of the six remaining Scottish banks. We had amalgamated with the Bank of Scotland and the National and the Commercial had joined forces by then.'

'What were the other three for?' I asked.

'One was for the Bank of England and the others for the larger denominations. Mind you, they weren't spreading all the time, they just had to fit it in between their other jobs.'

'Where did you put the dollars?' I asked, trying to sound intelligent.

'Oh, we had a separate till for them,' he said. 'They came in enormous quantities, especially from the bookies, and we gave a flat rate of seven shillings to the dollar. We worked unpaid overtime every night I was there. The lad from Glasgow and I might manage to take a short walk before we went to bed, but that's all we saw of Dunoon and the manager worked harder than we did. I didn't envy him his job. I only had about three weeks of it and that was quite enough.'

Though he didn't covet that particular manager's job, he was now well into his forties, had had a lot of experience taking charge of branches for short periods and had twice been in Head Office for intensive training in trustee and executry work and in foreign exchange. He knew Mr Sim had been giving him excellent reports yet still the longed-for branch of his own seemed as far away as ever. Then one day he was given a date for an interview in

Glasgow. The grapevine buzzed and we heard that Gourock was about to become vacant and that several of his contemporaries had also been asked to attend for interview. This was unusual. Normally the first thing a new manager knew about his appointment was the letter telling him when and where he was to start.

It was then, of all unfortunate times, at least fifteen years after the war, that Iain's neck broke out into a horrible crop of boils and blisters that he recognised as being very similar to those that had resulted from the application of mustard gas. Whether this was the cause was never established, though as the Blood Transfusion Service would still not accept his 'contaminated' blood, it seemed possible that the gas was still in his system. Whatever the explanation, he certainly was not at his best for the trip to Glasgow. The interviewers were sympathetic, but it was clear that he would not be going to Gourock! However, before he left he was asked, 'Mr Rattray, if you had a choice, where in the country would you like to go?'

He was so astonished by this question that he answered it without consideration at all and completely honestly. 'I don't care where I go, so long as it's by the sea.' They smiled at his frankness and asked if he sailed. 'No,' he said. 'It's just that I grew up by the sea, and a town without the sea is like a sitting-room without a fire – it's got no focus.'

Sophisticated he was not; but his straight answer seems to have done no harm, as when the all-important letter did arrive, about a year later, it told him that he had been appointed as manager at

Tarbert, where the bank house is just across the road from the sea. (Iain was much amused to discover that this letter was addressed to J.M. Rattray *Esq.* – hitherto he had been plain Mr!)

Before he left he had the opportunity to say good-bye to his favourite customer, old Dougall MacDougall. He was a retired farmer who acted as Registrar of Births, Marriages and Deaths at Kilmartin. In his youth he had driven cattle along the old drove roads from Ford to Falkirk Tryst – right across Scotland. If they got a good price they treated themselves and took the train to Glasgow where they caught the boat at the Broomielaw to take them back to Ardrishaig. From there the walk home was a mere fourteen miles or so. If the prices were poor they walked the whole way!

Dougall was one of nature's gentlemen and his visits to the bank were a delight. As soon as he entered the door he doffed his hat and greeted the senior lady, 'Good-morning, Miss MacVicar,' and gave her a little bow. Then he turned to the junior, 'Good-morning, Miss Gillies,' and she received her little bow. Then he approached the counter and put his hand through the grill to shake hands with the teller, 'Good-morning, Mr Rattray.' Only then did he open his coat and extract the cheque he wanted Iain to cash.

He was one of those chosen to meet the Queen on her first visit to Oban. People now just won't believe the weather we had that day. The gale was such that the launch couldn't approach the quay and a hastily constructed affair made of fish boxes had to be devised in a slightly more sheltered spot. The rain came down in sheets without let up and conditions couldn't have been worse, but the Queen went through with the programme in spite of it all. When Dougall was presented, he took her hand warmly in both of his, 'It's good to see you here safely, my lassie!' he said.

When Iain got to Tarbert, he found that one of Dougall's sons was a customer there and now, in old age and eighty miles from Kilmartin, we have his great-granddaughter as one of our nearest neighbours. Life is like that in Argyll.

9

Tarbert as Manager – Learning the Ropes

We had always known that we could be moved anywhere in Scotland at very short notice. I found the idea rather exciting, and I think my daughter did too. By the time the move came she was in her second year at The Mount, a Quaker School in York where she had a bursary, so that although she was delighted at the news, it was going to make no difference to her education. David was another matter. He didn't want to go. He didn't want to leave his friends and he didn't want to leave Lochgilphead – full stop.

'It's not that far away David,' we coaxed, 'and it's a lovely big house and it's got a telephone and soon we'll be able to have a car. It's right beside the harbour and you'll be able to watch the boats and the lorries. You'll soon make new friends...' It was no good. In the end the promise that we would hire a television extracted a reluctant compliance but he still was not happy. There wasn't anything we could do about it, but it was worrying.

However, he had plenty of time to get used to the idea as Walter Greenlees, Iain's predecessor in Tarbert, had been moved to Renfrew where there was no bank house. So his wife could not move out until a suitable home had been found in the Renfrew area. This gave us several months to prepare for the move but Iain had just a week to find people to take over all his voluntary jobs; never an easy task. It is odd, but it is taken for granted that bank staff will contribute their expertise freely and take on treasurerships of charitable and voluntary organisations without thought of reward, but tradesmen who serve on committees don't think twice about putting in a bill for any work they do.

For some months Iain travelled daily on Craig's bus, but during an unexpected spell of snowy weather, he stayed at the Castle Hotel and, until we finally moved, he took his lunch there. For the first, and only, time in our married lives I knew when to expect him for his evening meal, but finishing on the dot didn't suit Iain's way of working and he couldn't wait to move into the house.

However, it didn't take long for him to settle in what he still thought of as Mr Couper's room, though it took longer for him to believe that he was really in charge. Some of the customers he already knew and, during the first week, he was visited by a customer from Gigha.

'Oh, it's yourself, man,' he said as they settled in the manager's room. 'I was glad to hear it was you that got it,' and he took a half-bottle out of his pocket. 'You'll have a dram?'

Walter had warned him, 'Look, I don't know whether you drink or not and it's none of my business, but if you've any sense you're a non-drinker as far as Tarbert is concerned. If you accept a drink from one you'll have to accept drinks from them all or they'll be offended, but nobody is going to do business with a banker who drinks. The only safe thing is to say no to everyone!'

Iain wouldn't have accepted a drink in the office in any case, so he refused gently and after the customer had left he went along to the Castle Hotel for his lunch. As he passed through the bar he was greeted by several customers and, as usual he declined their offers of a drink, and was grateful for Walter's timely advice. The dining room was empty except for the Skipness minister, Mr Green, and his mother. They invited Iain to join them and Mr Green at once asked, 'Would you like a drink, Mr Rattray?' Iain was foxed. He didn't really want a drink, but it was the minister and he didn't want to look as if he was trying to be holier than he was. Anyway, there was no-one else in the room, so reluctantly he responded. 'Well. Yes, please, just a small one.' Mr Green picked up the jug on the table and poured him a small glass of water!

Miss MacVicar had been sent as teller to Tarbert about a year earlier and the apprentice, John McIntyre, was the Lochgilphead police inspector's son and, as a schoolboy, had delivered our groceries in Lochgilphead, so Iain knew the staff already. His spells doing relief had made him fairly familiar with the office. But he realised he still had much to learn.

The business at Tarbert depended mainly on the fishing, though the branch had farming customers from Kilberry and Skipness and as far down the Kintyre peninsula as Tayinloan, as well as on the islands of Gigha and Jura. Ever mindful of the need to be able 'to put a face on every signature' he set about getting to know them all. He already had a fair knowledge of farming finance and the problems of the tourist industry but fishing was new and it was vital that he should get to know the fishermen and learn to understand their needs if he was to make a success of his time in Tarbert.

He was lucky in his mentors. 'Old' Tommy Jackson had been at sea all his life. Now retired, once he realised that Iain really wanted to learn, he was ready to spend as much time as it took to pass on his store of information. The family owned two boats which were skippered by his nephews; and he had been one of the original partners of MacFarlane and Jackson, the fish salesmen. His son had now taken over and was partnered by Jack Dawson the dynamic auctioneer. Jack managed all the fishermen's financial affairs. He sold the fish, paid the boats' accounts, worked out the share due to each fisherman and had the money made up for the skippers to pay out at the end of the week.

Soon after Iain arrived the fishermen went on to PAYE and each Saturday morning Jack phoned Iain a list of boats, the names of the crews and the amount each had earned. Then Iain worked out the tax due and phoned back. Each boat paid a nominal £5 a year for this service. It was not going to make him rich but the process helped him to become familiar with the individual names in each crew and he soon learned to put a face on them.

In the early sixties the herring fishing was good and the fishermen were doing well. It was said that an incomer was told 'It doesn't matter whether you're a £60 a week fisherman or a £1000 a year professional – we're all the same in Tarbert.' When you work it out the fishermen were earning about three times as much as the professional! Iain had a basic salary of £1500 when he was first appointed to Tarbert.

Boats came in to discharge their catches from Girvan and the other Ayrshire ports, as well as from Carradale and Campbeltown, and he soon learned to recognise the registration numbers painted at the front of the boats. As soon as the fish was auctioned it was loaded into huge lorries and most of it was rushed off to the central belt, though some went on to London.

A number of these lorries were owned by Ben Mundell who had an office on the corner of the bank building and he knew everything and everyone. Once he had accepted Iain, he became an invaluable source of information. Iain, as he came out of the bank, would stop for the usual polite greeting and Ben would tug his ear and say 'I'm hearing...' and what he heard was invariably reliable.

Ben spent a lot of his time standing at the door of his office in an old overcoat and fingerless mittens looking as if he hadn't two halfpennies to rub together, but he was one of the most prosperous tradesmen in the district, and one of the shrewdest, and he had contacts all over the county. At that time, before the advent of the 'roll-on, roll-off' ferries, people going to Gigha, Jura, Islay or Colonsay on holiday often chose to leave their cars at the West Loch and pick them up on their return. They would leave their keys and Ben would send drivers to move them into his own garage for safe keeping and take them back to meet the boats on their owner's return.

Often he didn't have drivers available if they were away with fish lorries or with hired cars, and on these occasions Ben would commandeer anyone with a driving licence. The boat sailed during the bank's lunch hour and frequently John McIntyre was roped in to help. Ben would look in to the bank just before it closed and dangle a bunch of keys. 'What'll you have this time?' he would ask, 'A Ford, a Morris or a Rover? Take your pick.' Eventually the day came when Iain was coaxed into helping out too, and he helped several times before Ben's wife found out. Mrs Mundell was horrified. 'Whatever were you thinking about? You can't have the banker driving your cars for you! What will folk say?'

Actually, Iain quite enjoyed it, but Ben didn't dare ask him again.

The boatyard, too, was active at that time. At least one fishing boat was launched and the new ferry for Colintraive, as well as smaller yachts and pleasure craft, but mainly it was used for repairs. Leitch, the sailmaker, had a thriving business which continues under his son, but the boatyard folded long ago.

I have tried very hard to get Iain to describe how it felt to have his own branch after so long and what difference it made but all he will say is: 'Well it wasn't all that different really. I'd been deputising for other managers for years. I suppose the best thing was knowing that I wasn't going to be sent off on relief at a moment's notice any more and I could begin to plan ahead. I could get to know the customers better, too. As a teller I could chat over the counter but there wasn't much time for more than pleasantries. Now I could invite them into the room and chat for an hour or so and really get to know them.'

He soon adopted Mr Munro's habit of 'going visiting'.

'I did tell the others where I was going and roughly when I hoped to be back; but if I was going to call on one farmer and I was passing another customer on the way, I would drop in for a chat and see if they needed anything.'

Head Office intervened very little. The inspectors told him, 'It's your office. We don't want to hear from you unless something is going wrong.' Like all other managers, he had a limit beyond which he could not lend without clearing it with Inspectors' department, but they were unlikely to turn down a loan if he had put up a sound case for it. Only really enormous loans went before the Board of Directors.

However, at the time Iain arrived in Tarbert the Credit Squeeze was in full force. Even established customers offering full security would be refused any sum over £100 and existing creditors were required to reduce their overdrafts by ridiculous amounts. It was not a good time to be a bank manager and only the fact that it was the same in all the banks prevented the customers from leaving in droves. There was nothing the individual banker could do about it except try to explain the position and go through the customers' accounts to see if they could find any slack that could be tightened up.

'The really maddening thing was,' said Iain, 'that sometimes, if they were really stuck, I could arrange a loan through a local hire purchase company. They could lend and I couldn't, no matter how much I wanted to. It was ridiculous.'

It helped that *The Agreements and Understandings* among the Banks in Scotland, ensured that all the banks paid the same rates of interest on deposits and that all their charges were similarly based. It was understood that they would not poach each other's customers but that incomers or new accounts were fair game.

This meant that they could compete only on the personality of the manager and his staff and the level of service they were prepared to offer.

There were several managers of the Clydesdale Bank in Tarbert while we were there. MacGregor-Smith (we can't remember ever hearing his Christian name, everyone just called him Mac!) was in charge when Iain arrived. He was probably the most idiosyncratic of all the agents Iain had met and he referred to himself as 'The People's Friend'. He seemed to make up his own rules as he went along and people either thought the world of him or they had no time for him; but he was a very able man. He was nearing retirement when Iain arrived and was inclined to be helpful to 'the young fella'. Mac's great interest was his beautiful garden. He had bought a villa at the end of Pier Road and had created a masterpiece which was really special and which he had floodlit at night. The Clydesdale had a small modern office in the centre of the village, but it did not have a bank house at that time.

Thus Mac's successor, Bill Walker, did not stay long as he had a wife and family and was unable to find somewhere to live. This was a pity as he and Iain got on well. He was a large cheery man and the Tarbert people soon began to talk about the 'big' banker and the 'wee' banker with equal respect and amusement. Most people had accounts in both branches and it was not unknown for the occasional smart boy to try to play off one against the other. That this didn't work was largely due to some very discreet but mutually understood conversations between the two bankers. All in all it was a very civilised way of running a business.

Iain continued to be the wee banker along with the wee doctor and the wee minister. They were all small men, but they worked well together and were able to do quite a bit of good by stealth between them.

All new managers were given a week's training in Edinburgh during their first year and, in due course, Iain's turn came up and he joined five other new appointees in a small hotel on the outskirts of the capital. The purpose of the exercise was to introduce them to the various Head Office officials with whom they were dealing. Iain and another West of Scotland manager spent an interesting day in the Inspectors' department in Glasgow. The other four, being from the East of Scotland, met the Edinburgh inspectors.

They had one session 'in a wee room in the Premises department', where they were introduced to the provisions of the new 'Shops and Premises Act, 1962' which was pretty boring stuff, enlivened only by a question from one of the East coast men.

'What are you going to do when Beeching closes the station at Kittybrewster?'

For some reason this obviously threw the speaker, who got very red and blustered, 'Plans are being prepared,' and rapidly moved on.

The rest were puzzled by this and as soon as they settled for lunch someone asked, 'What was all that about Kittybrewster Station?'

The Kittybrewster agent grinned and said, 'In Kittybrewster, the petty cash provides pennies for the staff to use the facilities in the station – there are none in the office.'

It seemed incredible but later, on holiday in Aberdeen, we saw that branch. It was a very small but very busy office on a restricted site close to the Auction Mart and the station. Iain thought it probably dated back to the small local bank that had been swallowed up by the Union Bank at the end of the last century. It was a good site but there was little room for extension.

At the end of the course they were honoured by being invited to lunch in the Directors' dining room. At the end, Prince Charles' snuffbox was passed round.

'At least, I think they said Prince Charles. It was something to do with the Jacobites,' said Iain, who had been less than impressed by the occasion. He was far more interested and amused to find that even in the upper echelons of the bank it was easy to detect which men had always been Bank of Scotland and those who were old Union Bank men. The latter clearly thought that the Union Bank was far superior.

Thus Iain was fairly well established in Tarbert before the rest of us moved down. The bank house became available to us during the summer term but, inadvisedly as it turned out, we decided to let David finish his school year in Lochgilphead. This proved to be a great mistake, as he spent the summer worrying about starting in a new school. One morning in the new school and he had made friends with the son of the Co-operative manager across the road and all his worries were forgotten. Had we been wiser he might have had Hugh's company all through the holiday and we would all have been saved a deal of anxiety.

I had been on the County Committee of the Red Cross so I had some contacts in Tarbert and the tradesmen's wives were very welcoming. Although we still attended Friends' Meetings on Sunday afternoons when we could, we started to attend the Parish Church, as Iain had inherited the job of church treasurer and the new minister, Bill Eadie, and his wife Helen had made us so welcome from the start. Helen persuaded me to go to the Women's Guild where I made more friends and I soon began to love Tarbert as much as Iain did.

10
Tarbert – A Man of Many Parts

In spite of the agreement between the banks, a manager was judged by the increase in business done by the branch. Since poaching from the opposition was frowned on, he had to attract business from people who didn't currently have an account in either bank. In a small place where everything was known this meant that the banker must be seen to be sympathetic and approachable, on good terms with everyone but not party to any cliques. Everyone's friend, but not 'one of the boys' as no-one wants a lightweight bank manager. It was not an easy line to tread, but after so many years in the service it was one that seemed to come naturally to Iain, as it did to most country managers at that time.

The traditional way of getting known was to serve on voluntary committees and he inherited several of these from Walter Greenlees. Being treasurer of the Church of Scotland brought him into contact with the elders and the Congregational Board and thus to most of the leading shopkeepers and tradesmen in the village. But while he was getting to know them, they were watching to see how he handled the church's affairs and drawing their own conclusions. It was a two-way process.

It was much the same with the Clyde Fishermen's Association, though this post carried a small remuneration. He would have taken it on even if it did not as there were so many customers and prospective customers among the fishermen.

A small group of local businessmen were trying hard to boost Tarbert and to this end had invested in the local cinema. Walter had acted as company secretary and virtually ran the operation, paying the staff, balancing the books, dealing with entertainment tax and ordering the films. This, also, was an additional source of income that Iain inherited from his predecessor. Another group, with some overlap, ran Tarbert Projects Ltd which, among other things, organised a guide book for Tarbert. This was a much smaller operation and carried no salary but he took it over with the rest of Walter's little jobs.

Iain was not a bowler but he found that he was honorary secretary and treasurer of Tarbert Bowling Club. It was not an onerous job except for the one day in the year when they held their Annual Fête. However, though he was a keen golfer, the Clydesdale manager held that job. He was sorry about that as it was one well worth having since practically everyone played golf. Certainly, most of the men in the bank were golfers, and so were many of the women. Among the customers at Tarbert was an eighty-year-old pensioner of the bank, who told Iain quite seriously, 'I'm afraid I'm going to have to give up the golf. I read in the paper this morning that more men die on the golf course than die on a rugby pitch!'

Iain hadn't the heart to point out that not many men continued to play rugby in their old age. The old man continued to play a few holes regularly and died happily in his armchair by the fire!

It was Bill Walker of the Clydesdale Bank who founded the Toastmasters in Tarbert and Iain was one of his first recruits so it is obvious that the competition for influence was hardly cut-throat! Bill was the first President, so Iain was the natural choice for treasurer and so the account went to the Bank of Scotland, but the account, as such, was worth very little from the banks' point of view and both managers had the same opportunity to make contacts. The two men were on good terms and they co-operated in all sorts of ways in spite of the fact that the terms of their employment meant that the manager was never officially off-duty. He was expected to pursue the bank's interest at all times. Nevertheless, as far as these two bankers were concerned, the Toastmasters simply provided a good night out in agreeable company.

One practical outcome of Bill's initiative was that Tarbert was one of the few small places we have known where there was never any difficulty in finding someone to propose a vote of thanks! The most unlikely people found that, with practice, they could speak well and fluently and most had interesting tales to tell.

One man, who had a ship-chandler's shop spoke about the local nick-names, most of which went back for generations and could be used to differentiate different branches of the same family. For example, the MacDougalls were divided into the 'Tars' and the 'Toms'. The speaker, whose surname was Smith, was Johnnie Rawt, which he said was derived from 'Rhodes', as an ancestor of his had apparently borne a marked resemblance to the famous Cecil Rhodes. The other branch of the Smiths [from which the former leader of the Labour Opposition was descended] were the 'Hairies'. No-one could remember why, but presumably an earlier

John Smith had had a good beard!

As the business increased, Iain came to feel that they could use another member of staff. Now that banking is computerised it is hard to believe that in those days managers in rural branches typed their own letters (usually with two fingers) and all the arithmetic in the office was done mentally. At the time of the monthly balance they were really hard-pressed and as the Clydesdale had an adding machine they had been borrowing it one day a month ever since MacGregor-Smith's time. Iain knew he wouldn't have a chance of getting an additional member of staff and he suspected a straight request for an adding machine would prove unfruitful. However, one day when we were on holiday in Edinburgh he went to pay a courtesy call to Head Office and called in on the staff manager.

As he had expected, his request for an additional member of staff was turned down flat.

'Yes, I do see the difficulty,' he said, emoliently, 'but we really are very busy and the staff are hard-pressed, especially at balance time. Do you think we could have an adding machine?'

'No, I'm afraid that's out of the question,' was the stony reply.

'Oh, well,' replied Iain philosophically, playing his trump card, 'we'll just have to go on borrowing the Clydesdale's!'

'What!' spluttered the horrified official. 'You can't do that – it's unthinkable.'

'I don't know about that, they've been doing it for the last ten years,' said the bold boy.

'Well, it must stop at once! I'll think about it!' The poor man was shocked to the core, but Iain got his adding machine.

Iain had been treasurer of the Lifeboat Fund in Lochgilphead and as the collection in Tarbert had fallen into abeyance he was prevailed upon to revive the Tarbert Branch. This was a popular move in a fishing community and donations were always generous.

At one point he held no fewer than thirteen treasurerships. I used to complain that he had too much on his plate, but they were not all equally onerous and as he said, 'They don't all come to the boil at once!' This was true. The Horticultural Society, like the Bowling Club, had one annual event, but it was hectic while it lasted. We were all astonished at the amount of work and organisation that was involved. Iain Macintyre, the greengrocer next door, was the secretary and the main burden of the work fell on him. The schedules had to be drawn up and circulated in advance. They were never quite the same as last year and the minor alterations were the result of considerable discussion, not to say argument, as feelings could run high. New classes for flower arrangement might be added and certain unpopular vegetable classes dropped, but only over someone's dead body!

The night before the event, the stands were recovered from the shed at the back of Macintyre's shop and transported to the village hall where the men erected them and the women covered them with clean white paper. This was no five-minute task as there were four lines of tables running the length of the hall and each table had a second tier at the back so that the hundreds of exhibits could be properly displayed.

The day itself was a glorious example of ordered chaos. It really was impressive, albeit exhausting. A dozen or so judges went round the vegetables and flowers, the baking and preserves, the floral arrangements and the children's exhibits accompanied by the children of the committee members who ran back with the names of the first, second and third in each class to the clerical team in the committee rooms. They patiently noted them all down and wrote the names on the envelopes containing the small money prizes that Iain had made up. He then placed them in order so that the lengthy prize-giving would run smoothly. On top of that he had to count the marks to discover the best in each class and the best in the show so that the major cups and trophies went to the right competitors. Imagine the hassle if the competitors did their own arithmetic and he was proved to be wrong! Those marks were checked and double-checked as if they were competing for the National Lottery!

In the afternoon the crowds came. The takings had to be counted, and the raffle tickets sold and folded. Ice cream and teas provided more income, and more work, and when it was all over the hall had to be returned to its former pristine condition before the exhausted committee could call it a day. Everyone knew what they had to do and the thing went like clockwork. It was a masterpiece of organisation and in the years we were there it all went off with great good humour. All the family and any visitors who were staying with us were roped in and none of us would have missed it for anything! When it was all over, Iain would shut himself in the office and count and sort and bag the money, while the rest of us put our feet up, not altogether sorry that our offers of help had been turned down.

Tarbert was divided in two by a burn which marked the old parish boundaries. It ran under the road into the harbour just across the road from the bank. Thus the bank itself was in Kintyre but the shops across the corner were in Mid-Argyll. The church was on one side of the burn and the manse on the other. Because of this, the Tarbert folk felt that they did not get a square deal from either Kintyre District Council or the Mid-Argyll Council as they were peripheral in both cases. It has to be remembered that at that time Lochgilphead, which was no bigger than Tarbert, had its own Provost and Town Council, whereas the northern half of Tarbert was lumped in with Ardrishaig and the rural area surrounding Lochgilphead as far as Inveraray to form Mid-Argyll. The southern half of Tarbert was tacked on to the rest of Kintyre, which was focused on Campbeltown, though Campbeltown itself, like Lochgilphead, had its own Provost and Council. It didn't help when historians pointed out that Tarbert at one time had been a royal burgh with a charter from Robert the Bruce, as the charter had long been lost!

To remedy their perceived neglect, the local people set up Tarbert Ratepayers and elected a committee to lobby their representatives on both District Councils and on Argyll County Council. For once Iain was not the treasurer, in this case he was the secretary and in this role he maintained a lively correspondence with the statutory bodies on behalf of his fellow ratepayers. [In point of fact, he didn't pay any rates himself, the bank paid them for him, but as the whole thing had no official status anyway it didn't occur to him or to anyone else that he was disqualified.

After all he was the bank's full-time representative and the bank paid rates.]

The big issues at the time were street lighting and the state of the roads. The latter was a perennial problem in Argyll, where the ratio of miles of road per head of population is probably higher than anywhere else in the UK. The issue of street lighting was highlighted at that time, because Lochgilphead being on a trunk road had been given new lights all along the front under a Scottish Office scheme. The Tarbert people thought their need was greater because of the proximity of the harbour to the main street. People were unlikely to fall into the sea at Lochgilphead as there was a wide green between the road and the water, and the tide was out half the time anyway. In Tarbert, the possibility of falling into the harbour was real, especially after a few drinks. Unfortunately, the trunk road swung north towards Oban after it left Lochgilphead so the road to Campbeltown did not qualify for government assistance and, apart from the lights provided by the Harbour Authority at the quay, the lighting in both Ardrishaig and Tarbert was not what it could have been. It was a sore point!

Road surfacing was undertaken by the District Councils and one ridiculous result of this was that when Mid-Argyll resurfaced their share of the road, they finished it off so that a precise line ran across at the boundary and there it stopped, right in the middle of the village. By the time Kintyre got down to doing their half, the first half needed doing again! It was all great fun and the letters flowed fast and furious but to no great effect. Local efforts to do something about a playing field did eventually produce results, but long after Iain had moved on.

A bank manager in a city office left his work behind when he returned to his suburban home at night. His neighbours and golf or bridge partners were most unlikely to be his customers and he could lay down his bank manager persona with his city suit. In the country that was just not possible. The bank manager was never off duty. Quite often, Iain would arrange to see a fisherman on Saturday afternoon if the boats had been landing at Mallaig or Girvan all week; and the money from the cinema would be taken in on Saturday nights. But usually the local people didn't take advantage.

However, on one holiday Monday Iain took a call from a very arrogant holidaymaker who stayed regularly in a local 'big house'. He explained that the bank was closed but the speaker demanded to speak to the manager, he needed attention! We overheard Iain speaking in his 'stupid native' voice, 'Oh, I wouldna know onything about that – they're a' away – I'm juist the cleaner, ye ken', and he banged down the phone.

'What was all that about?' I asked.

'It was that arrogant so-and-so from up the road. He wanted me to open up to cash a cheque and he's not even a customer. I couldn't open the safe with only one key if I wanted to, but I'd have cashed it from my own money rather than see him stuck if he'd been half-way polite. I bet he wouldn't dream of asking his own bank to open up on a bank holiday. There'd be no-one there anyway, he was just trying it on.'

But we did get some odd calls. One day Barbara Jane answered the ring and came back looking very puzzled. 'Daddy, I think it's for you, but perhaps it's for Ben Mundell. I think the man said he wants a golden mini but I think he's foreign and I couldn't make it out.'

Iain said, 'Well there's no-one in Tarbert with a golden mini but I'll go and talk to him.'

Some time later he returned, helpless with laughter.

'It was the Dutchman, and it wasn't a golden mini, it was golden money he wanted. He was trying to buy some sovereigns but it took us a long time to get there. We don't keep them but I was able to tell him what to do – I think! Neither of us could understand the other.'

We heard no more about it so we hoped the Dutchman was successful in his quest.

In Tarbert the Church of Scotland held an evening service and if we were not at the service one of the elders would bring down the day's collections and hand them in to Iain for safe keeping. As Tarbert Church depended entirely on direct giving for the support of the church and drew the line at sales of work and similar fund-raising events, these collections contained a considerable amount. Iain couldn't put the money in the safe as two keys were necessary to open it and he held only one, but he could open the strong room and put it in there for the night. I was amused to find that when Iain was away on a course they handed it in to me, as usual. If it wasn't safe overnight in the care of a six-foot man I couldn't see that it was any safer in the care of a five-foot woman and I didn't have a key to the strong room. I just did what they could have done themselves, put it in a locked cupboard and hoped for the best. They, no doubt, felt much better knowing that it was safely 'in the bank'.

In a small place like Tarbert, people tended to turn to the banker for advice that wouldn't necessarily be regarded as banking in a city. The tradition of the lawyer-agent still lingered and, for example, the banker often acted as an insurance agent. When a manager was appointed he passed the first year's commissions on to his predecessor as payment for the business and after that the insurance business was a welcome addition to his basic salary. This was changed some years later and the bank took over all insurance business, the manager being given a suitable rise in salary to compensate him for the loss of earnings and I think most of the men welcomed the change. Apart from that, however, Iain always saw his role as being equivalent to that of a GP: 'Most routine things I can help them with, but if I can't, I can pass them on to a broker, or an accountant, or a lawyer or whatever.'

Some customers would ask him to make an appointment for them to see a lawyer in his office, or to arrange for a home visit, as the nearest law practices were in Lochgilphead and Campbeltown. Therefore he came to see even more of A.I.B. Stewart than he had done in Lochgilphead and quite often worked closely with him. On one occasion, one of Iain's customers had died and, as frequently happened, he had named him as his executor. Thus he was present at the reading of the will, which was not at all to the widow's liking.

'Be hanged to that for a tale!' she said, 'Tear it up and I'll tell you what to put.'

She had been the dominant force in her family all her life and was furious to learn that her husband, probably for the first and only time, had made up his own mind. She would not accept that there was nothing she could do about it.

But, at least he had left a will. All too often people didn't and this could cause great distress when, as could happen, what the law said and what everyone knew were the deceased wishes simply did not coincide.

Other people didn't even keep a bank account. On one occasion David Fairbairn rushed into the bank, clearly shaken. 'Mr Rattray, will you come down to the house with me. I'm finding money everywhere and I need a witness.' An old lady had died, apparently without kin, and he had been sent to prepare her possessions for the displenishing sale. Iain joined him, and, as he told us much later, 'There was money everywhere, in drawers and wardrobes, under the mattress and under the carpet. I only hope we got it all, otherwise somebody would have a pleasant surprise after the sale. There were hundreds and hundreds of notes. We both checked and double-checked and brought it all back to the office and got it checked again. It took all morning and we were filthy by the time we were finished. I do wish people wouldn't do that, it's downright dangerous.'

Money can be very dirty. You can't wash notes but it's not unknown for a lodgement of change, say from a coal-merchant or a chimney sweep, to be tipped in the sink and washed before an attempt is made to bag it.

Many of the farmers relied on the services of a chartered

accountant to deal with their accounts and many of them used a particular Glasgow firm. The same man came down regularly and was well known in the bank, but the time came when a younger man took over. He was a perfect city gentleman, complete with bowler hat and rolled umbrella, and was the cause of some gentle amusement locally. Even Iain had to smile when he was told of the slight problem the young man had with his first set of farming accounts.

'It says here that you had so many sheep at the end of the year. Now you have all these extra, and I don't see anything to account for where they came from.'

'Well, now,' said the farmer, 'I'm thinking mebbe yir mither could explain that.'

By the end of 1968 we were well settled in. During our first year the bank had approved, and paid for, quite major improvements and redecoration in the house, and, in each subsequent year, we had been allowed to redecorate another room. We had just completed the redecoration of the final room and felt that, at last, we had things to our liking. The children were both away at school and Iain was as happy as a sandboy with good staff in the office and plenty to occupy him out of banking hours. He was fifty-four and we expected that we would remain where we were until he retired at sixty-five.

However I, at forty-three, was finding time heavy on my hands and had decided to respond to pleas for people in middle-life to train as teachers, as at that time there was a serious shortage of staff in the schools. This meant commuting to Jordanhill College in

Glasgow, spending Monday to Friday there and the weekends at home. It worked out better than we had dared to hope and eventually I hoped to join the staff in the Tarbert School.

On the second of January 1969, the office was open for a couple of hours in the morning. Iain was working in his room when he received a telephone call from Norval Charteris, manager at Campbeltown.

'Good news in the post this morning,' he said.

'Is there?' Iain said. 'We haven't had our mail yet. What's new?'

'I'm retiring and you're coming to succeed me. Congratulations!'

Somehow Iain found the words to express his thanks for the kind thought behind the call though he was shaken to his roots and then he rushed round to the Post Office to see if they would let him have the Head Office letter. It was right enough; he was to start in Campbeltown in ten days time, and Ian Bulloch was to take over Tarbert as well as Ardrishaig. It was a big promotion for them both, though neither of them had been seeking advancement and were perfectly happy where they were. But once he got over the shock he began to think that he might like Campbeltown. If he had to move, better Campbeltown than anywhere else.

11

Campbeltown – Council Finance

Such sudden moves were the rule in the bank at the time. Iain always assumed that the idea was to discourage the manager from fiddling the books, as he wouldn't have time to arrange a cover-up; but it made things difficult, especially in this case where his successor would not be living in Tarbert and already had more than his share of voluntary treasurerships in Ardrishaig. In the event, an accountant, Archie MacNeill, was appointed and he moved into the bank house and fell heir to many of the local activities previously undertaken by the manager. Even so, the week before Iain's departure was a nightmare, since, apart from making arrangements to hand over the books of a dozen different organisations and bringing his own work up-to-date, he had to take his successor round and introduce him to the customers.

One such visit, to Mrs Beavis of the Columba Hotel, was memorable. She took them into her sitting room and, as the three of them sat down, her pet Mynah bird settled down on her head. She took no notice and neither did Iain, as by this time he was used to the creature and was accustomed to seeing her wearing it on her head like a hat. Bulloch, however, couldn't take his eyes off it and indeed it must have been one of the most bizarre interviews he had ever experienced.

Iain laughed afterwards, 'I think the poor man wondered what on earth he was getting into!'

As it happened, the experiment of having the two branches

under one manager didn't last long as Ian Bulloch's health broke down, and, after a short spell running the Ardrishaig office only, he took early retirement. He must have been one of the most popular men in the bank and his early death saddened everyone.

Mr Charteris was staying on in Campbeltown, so he kept on most of his voluntary activities. The exception was the Lifeboat treasurership. Since there was a lifeboat stationed in Campbeltown the treasurer had to be always on the spot to pay the crew. Norval intended to do a lot of travelling and didn't want to be tied down. It was a very interesting job, though most of the responsibility was carried by the secretary. We were surprised to learn that it was not the coxwain, but the secretary, who made the decision to launch the lifeboat, the theory being that the men who actually sailed the boat would never, no matter what the conditions, refuse to take the boat out, but the occasion could arise when someone had to be realistic enough to say, 'No!' On the one week-end the secretary was away the responsibility passed to the treasurer and we were on pins the whole weekend. It was not a responsibility that Iain felt competent to carry, never having sailed a boat in his life!

Archie MacNeill took over the Tarbert office and he and his wife loved the place as much as we did. However, we couldn't move out of the house at once, as Norval Charteris was a widower and couldn't give his attention to finding a new home until he had got rid of his responsibilities to the bank. He stayed on in Campbeltown, where he had many friends, and found a pleasant flat in the town, but moving from a large house to a smaller one is much more difficult than moving to a larger place, as we were to discover for ourselves several years later.

Meanwhile, Iain moved into the Argyll Hotel and we met in the Tarbert house at weekends to plan the move and do the packing. At half-term the college gave me an extra week's leave and we were able to deal with the removal. The new house was quite separate from the bank and was a large stone villa overlooking Campbeltown Loch, just across the water from Craigard, where the children had been born. Barbara Jane was quite indignant about that. Filling in a form she complained, 'Place of birth – Campbeltown. Present address – Campbeltown. You'd think I'd never been anywhere else!' But they liked Woodside and it was a good place to bring their friends on holiday.

It had a huge garden, which was fine if you had time to look after it, but it was a bit of a burden in the circumstances. Everyone Iain met said, 'I hope you like gardening?' and then added, 'Did you know Mr Smith? He was a wild man in the garden!'

Mr Smith had been Norval's predecessor in the house and Iain knew of him. He was a nice big man but Iain couldn't help wondering what on earth he'd got up to, to get such a reputation.

However, when he mentioned this to me I was able to enlighten him, as I'd learned during my visits to Craigard for the births of the children that in Campbeltown 'wild' indicates that something is excessive and is pretty well interchangeable with 'very'.

'That's a wild tame dog he's got,' indicates that the dog is very tame. Mr Smith had been a very keen gardener and as long as we were in that house people spoke to us about him being 'a wild man in the garden'.

There was a large conservatory at the rear, heated by pipes leading from a back boiler behind the morning room fire. We grew splendid tomatoes, but the structure was a bit ramshackle and after one inspector's visit Iain came home and said,

'They say the conservatory is to come down.'

'Over my dead body,' I replied.

'That's what they're afraid of, my love,' he said dryly, but we managed to put off the evil day as long as we were in the house, though it was demolished as soon as we left.

It had been an enormous wrench to leave the house at Tarbert and we knew that Iain was now planning to retire at sixty (as house prices were rising at an alarming rate) so I never quite felt the same attachment to that house. It was more like an official residence and I was very aware that we were transient. We were quite separate from the office and, as I was away so much during the first three years and teaching in one of the outlying villages thereafter, Iain's life in the bank became separated from his home life almost as much as if he'd been a city banker.

Campbeltown had at one time been the biggest and most prosperous town in Argyll, with over twenty working distilleries and a large fishing fleet. It was the centre for a wide agricultural area which had provided grain for the distilleries and milk for a flourishing creamery. Farm land in Kintyre, particularly down the West coast and on the Laggan, i.e. the land between the town and Machrihanish, was far more productive than the land in Mid-Argyll. The large fertile fields were atypical in the Highlands and farming was much more profitable.

Nevertheless, by the time Iain arrived in 1969, only two distilleries remained and only one of them was actually producing whisky. The coal pit at Machrihanish, which had been reopened after the war, had finally closed two years earlier and the fishing fleet was in decline. And, although a new shipyard had recently been opened, as had a factory making men's clothing, the general impression was of a town in decline, in spite of the strenuous efforts that were being made by the Provost and the Town Council to attract new industry.

During the war, Campbeltown had been an important naval base and there was still a considerable presence of both the American and British Air Forces on the base at Machrihanish, said to be one of the few aerodromes with a runway capable of accommodating Concorde. In addition, the base provided a fair number of civilian jobs. One advantage of this facility, apart from the work it provided, was that it could be, and still is, used by a civilian airline to provide a twice-daily, week-day service to Glasgow. It is expensive, but the half-hour flight is wonderful in comparison with the tedious 150-mile journey by road. It is a beautiful run on a good day and tourists love it, but it does begin to pall after years of travelling. The regular sailings, which had previously been the chief method of transport, had been severely reduced and were soon discontinued.

Life at the end of this long peninsula had, in fact, many of the characteristics of island life, comparative isolation being matched by a community life that was, and still is, much stronger than that found in mainland towns of a similar size.

The Bank of Scotland was one of five banks in the town, the others being the Clydesdale, the Royal, the Commercial and a Savings Bank, the latter being regarded as 'not a proper bank' by the others as, at that time, it didn't operate cheque accounts or issue its own notes. There were five members of staff. Mr Grant, a widower in his late forties, was the accountant – a kindly and gentle man. None of the others had completed their bank exams but the two boys were well on the way, and the two girls were keen and efficient, so Iain felt that, once again, he had been very lucky in his staff. Though the staff changed over the years, it was always a happy office.

As in Tarbert, he started by trying to get to know his customers. Norval Charteris took him to visit customers at Southend and at Carradale, where the bank opened a sub-office weekly in one of the bungalows. [The Clydesdale and the Royal also paid weekly visits to Carradale.] Then, to the surprise of the staff, he insisted on spending a week on the counter and another week doing the ledgers to get the feel of the business and to get to know the names and faces of as many people as he could. His own work was done after the doors closed.

It helped that his own office, a mere glassed-in cubby hole compared with his large room at Tarbert, was on the customers' side of the counter. Whenever he heard an unfamiliar voice he would nip out and Kenneth McConnachie, a very popular local teller, would introduce him to the customer – so that in those early days a lot of his time was spent 'just talking to customers'. He made a special point of being out of his office on the 25th of the month when the milk credits came in from the Milk Marketing Board, and on sale days, as these were the days when the farmers were likely to be in and he wanted to be readily available to any of them who wanted to discuss the state of their overdraft. The reason that the farmers had overdrafts was not that the farmers were in difficulty – far from it. It came about because up to the late 1950s all the land in Kintyre had been owned by the Duke of Argyll, but he was forced, as the result of accumulating death-duties, to offer the farms for sale to the sitting tenants. Thus all the farmers in the district changed from tenant farmers to farm owners at the same time and they all took out mortgages to make this possible and were still paying them off when Iain took over the branch.

In an odd way, this sense of 'all being in the same boat' added to the social cohesion. This was already very strong, since they were all descended from Ayrshire farmers who had been brought over to take over the tenancies when a previous Duke of Argyll had reorganised the farms more than a century before. They had been intermarrying ever since, so that they had bonds of relationship as well as a shared occupation.

Iain soon decided that he liked the Campbeltown folk. They came in greater variety than in Tarbert. There were fewer fishermen, and they were spread around the banks, but he knew enough about fishing by now to be at ease with the fishermen among his own customers. There were more, and more varied, shops and more hotels and public houses and the population of between six and seven thousand was served by two large primary schools and a large comprehensive Grammar School, so that there were many more teachers. The newly developing shipyard provided an interesting challenge and he enjoyed helping several small firms of tradesmen to get started, but his work was more strictly confined to banking than it had been in Tarbert. There were three firms of lawyers, one of chartered accountants and two or three insurance businesses, so that he wasn't expected to be an all-purpose financial adviser in quite the same way as he had been before. Nevertheless, for quite a number of people the banker was the first port of call if they needed advice, and this was the part of his work that he most enjoyed. At that time none of the banks would have considered charging for this service.

Sadly, we have become accustomed in recent years to watching television accounts of the closure of mines and factories, and invariably the point is made that not only will the redundant workers feel the pinch, but there will also be a knock-on effect in the surrounding area. In a self-contained community like Campbeltown, the effect is particularly marked and bankers, more than anyone, are in a position to watch the progress of damage done by the closure of a significant source of employment. The pit at Machrihanish had been closed for two years when Iain arrived, so he was not immediately confronted with problems on this scale, though he was very aware of the importance for the town of the survival of the remaining major employers. The distance from the markets was a great handicap to manufacturing industry, though firms making high value goods would be at an advantage as it is very difficult for thieves to get off the peninsula quickly, the more so as a telephone call can close the bridge at Ardrishaig, virtually turning Kintyre into an island. This has an effect on insurance premiums as the risk of loss is much reduced. Like the other bankers in the town, Iain was in contact with the Highlands and Islands Development Board who were continually trying to persuade potential incoming industries of these advantages.

The interdependence of the community, however, is evident to a banker on a normal day-to-day basis.

'Imagine,' Iain said, 'we have a garage proprietor "A" who wants to build an extension to his garage. He has not enough cash in hand but he has a lot of money outstanding. We have, in addition, a building contractor "B" and a painter "C" who are hoping to get the contract to build the extension but they need funds to buy materials and pay skilled workmen. So it all turns on the men who owe money to Mr A and the chances are that they will be farmers. Nothing can move until after the cattle sales, when Mr A will approach the farmers and tell them that his terrible bank manager is pressing for repayment and could they possibly pay something off their accounts? Being decent chaps they will all oblige and he can set the wheels in motion. He pays B and C – they pay their suppliers and their workmen, who spend at least some of the money locally, so the money goes round and around and keeps everyone happy! But the banker can see the whole picture.'

Incidentally, Iain was always amused that, in fictional accounts, bank managers are always fearsome ogres and bank clerks are always wimps. 'I've always wondered,' he said, 'how on earth they thought we changed overnight from spineless clowns to overbearing bullies!'

The biggest account in Campbeltown, however, was not a private or business customer but Argyll County Council. Iain was not new to the working of the council. After all it was the council's influence that had led to the opening of the branch in Oban where he had started his apprenticeship. In Lochgilphead he had to deal with the accounts of the police, the County Engineer's department and the County Clerk's office, so he knew how the system worked. However, in Argyll, it was policy for the various county offices to be spread around the county as so much employment was involved and Campbeltown had the Finance department.

The Campbeltown branch had had the account for so long that a very smooth system had evolved between the bank and the Finance department and, in particular, between Ewen Longmuir, the County Treasurer, and Norval Charteris. Iain just took over where Norval had left off. Each day thirty or forty credit transfers would pass through the Campbeltown office to various parts of the county.

If the county had received a large payment, for example a grant from the Scottish Office for major road-works or housing, and didn't require to use it immediately, it was put to work earning interest for the council. Usually it was lent to other county councils who were temporarily in need of it.

First thing in the morning Iain would receive a call from Ewen, 'Lend [say] £100,000 to Renfrew, for seven days, through [such and such a] bank, and £50,000 to Lanark for ten days.' The loans were always short-term, but when dealing in hundreds of thousands, or even millions, the interest was a significant part of the county's income. Iain would pass the figures to Mr Grant, who passed them on to his opposite number in London chief office. He and Mr MacIntyre had been doing this several times a week for years and had become friendly. London sophistication disappeared, and the conversation in broad Scots would begin, 'Oh, it's yourself – and how's the weather in Campbeltown today?' And a polite little exchange of pleasantries, Scottish fashion, would precede the matter of business. It was the routine moving around of large sums of money to earn the maximum interest for the council that led to the disastrous loss of Western Isles Council money in the BCCI affair!

The county's Annual Balance was an important day in the branch's year. As soon as the banks holding the various sub-accounts all over the county closed for the day, they would phone Campbeltown to transfer the total balance held in their branch to the central account held in Campbeltown. All the money held by the county had to be in the one account by the close of business on 15th May. Ewen would have let Iain have a list of the monies he was expecting, so that he could check the credits as they came in, and the Campbeltown branch didn't close its books that day until all the money was safely in the main account. The necessary paperwork followed by post, but the actual transfer of money was done over the phone after the bank had closed and it really was a hectic few hours. Nowadays, the whole thing is done very simply by computer, but they miss out on the interchange of news and bank gossip that accompanied the figures!

The charge demanded by the bank for this service was

'hammered out amicably over a cup of coffee in the old Poor-House between Ewen and myself. There was no competitive tendering in those days!' The Poor-House had been converted to council offices and the bank and the county council seem to have been quite happy to leave the negotiations to the two of them.

On one occasion when he was taking his turn on duty at the Bank of Scotland stand at the Highland Show at Ingliston, just outside Edinburgh, he got into conversation with another manager who dealt with the council account for his city area. During a pause between customers they grabbed a cup of coffee and the city man said, 'Tell me, you have the county account at Campbeltown, don't you?'

'Yes,' said Iain, guardedly, wondering what was coming next.

'Do you have any problems with it?'

'Problems? No,' said Iain. 'It runs like clockwork.'

'Well you wouldn't believe the hassles we have,' was the reply. 'How do you do it?'

Iain explained the system he and Ewan worked and the man shook his head. 'You don't know you're born,' he exclaimed. 'I'm putting in for a shift to the country!'

As Mr Munro used to say, 'It needs the personal touch. You can't beat the personal touch!'

12
The End of the Road – Decimalisation and Computerisation

The value of having a good personal relationship with the customer became evident during the prolonged postal strike which lasted from 20th January to 1st March 1971. It was imperative that the movement of cheques between branches should not be interrupted and a courier service was quickly set up to serve the central belt but the outlying areas presented difficulties. In the end it was arranged that Archie MacNeill would send his Head Office letter containing the cheques to Campbeltown by bus and that both the Tarbert and the Campbeltown letters would be put on the plane to Glasgow. Similarly, Glasgow would send out their letters with the morning plane. West Coast Motors, who were customers of the branch, ran buses to the plane and to Tarbert, and throughout the strike they carried these letters to and fro without charge.

It was unfortunate that decimalisation was planned to take effect on February 15th – right in the middle of the postal strike. For months Iain and John Grant of the Royal Bank had been giving talks to Women's Institutes and Guilds and to other voluntary organisations telling them how the change would work and answering questions about the relative prices in old and new money.

'We trekked around from one village to another with our baskets of groceries and price cards showing the prices in "old" and "new" money,' he said. 'People were worried that the prices would be subtly rounded-up, and I suppose to some extent that did happen, but it wasn't as bad as they feared. Many older people were very anxious about the change and were sure they would never learn to adapt, and for long afterwards you would see people earnestly converting the new currency back to something that they could recognise. "What is that in old money?" they would ask before they decided to buy.'

The bank had issued a manual outlining the various stages of the changeover and giving the dates by which these changes were to be made. Iain became aware of the existence of this book through references to it in various circulars; but he did not have one. Neither did Archie MacNeill. He phoned Glasgow Head Office and they promised to look into it, but the very next day he received a telephone call from Arrochar Station, 'There are two parcels sitting here. Is nobody going to pick them up?' Arrochar was 100 miles away, but some idiot had taken literally the instruction that the manuals were all to be sent by rail, as the post was not available, and Arrochar was the nearest railway station!

He phoned Archie MacNeill to tell him, but Archie was not best pleased.

'Look – I'm already working one short. I can't spare anyone to go rushing off to Arrochar. You've got a bigger staff than me, can't you send someone?' So in the end, one of the Campbeltown clerks was dispatched to make the 200 mile round trip. I don't expect he minded as it would be a welcome change from routine. When he actually studied the document, Iain was much relieved to discover that what he had been doing was pretty close to the instructions in the manual and he had little difficulty in getting into step with the other branches.

The banks closed for two days to effect the changeover. The individual accounts all had to be brought up to date in old money and balanced and then reopened in decimal currency. This meant that all outstanding cheques had to be processed, that is, they had to be returned to the branch where the account was held, and this had to be done on the same date throughout the country. The Royal Bank manager collected the cheques from all three banks (by this time the Royal and the Commercial banks had amalgamated) and drove with them to Tarbert. Archie MacNeill added his own and the Clydesdale's cheques and took them to Lochgilphead where they were picked up by a security van which had brought the Oban cheques and would pick up more en route for Glasgow. Cheques for the Campbeltown branches arrived by plane the next day, and the laborious business of converting all the accounts began.

It would all have been so much easier by post!

When this elaborate arrangement was set up Iain ventured to ask, 'And what happens if it snows?'

He was told firmly, 'Don't you dare even to think it.' But it was more than a possibility at that time of year and everyone breathed a huge sigh of relief when the process was complete.

New coins had been distributed well in advance, and thereafter it was simply a case of taking in old coins and paying out new ones until all the old money was out of circulation. Around this time a roll-on, roll-off ferry began to run between Campbeltown and Red Bay in Northern Ireland. As the coast of Antrim is a mere 14 miles from the tip of Kintyre, this was a much shorter crossing than that from Stranraer, but with the troubles in Northern Ireland it was not really a very a good time to initiate the new service. More people came from Ireland than wanted to travel in the opposite direction. Nevertheless, it gave a considerable boost to the tourist trade and the hotels and shops soon began to pay in Irish notes.

Again, by taking advantage of the good relationship he had with the purser on the ferry, Iain was able to avoid charging his customers for accepting these notes. Normally, these would have had to be taken out of circulation and sent to Glasgow and there was a small charge involved. However, he reckoned there would be another branch in Northern Ireland facing the same problem in reverse, so he arranged for the purser to take quantities of Irish notes across with him and exchange them over there for English/Scottish notes. They were equivalent in value but couldn't be issued in the 'wrong' country. He would have been responsible for the money if the purser had decided to decamp, but all his banking judgements were based on his knowledge of the customer and he was never let down.

A few years before, while we were still in Tarbert, there had been a tremendous storm and huge swathes of trees in forestry plantations all over the county had been blown down overnight. Enormous damage was done, and it took years to deal with the fallen trees. When the ferry started, an arrangement was made to send them over to a pulp mill in Northern Ireland. Large trailers arrived in Campbeltown and were sent over as and when there was a space on the ferry and this helped to keep the service viable.

Eventually, of course, there came a time when all the fallen wood had been disposed of and, as the situation in Ireland deteriorated, so the number of people using the ferry declined and, consequently, the service stopped.

[Efforts have been made from time to time to get it restarted but, until the cease-fire, there was no real hope as security considerations always loomed large. As the base at Machrihanish has closed down completely, and the employment situation is more desperate than ever, much hangs on efforts to increase the tourist potential of the area and it was a great relief to everyone when a new operator started a summer service to Ballycastle in 1997. Unfortunately, it didn't last, though there are hopes it may be revived in 2002.]

Exchange control was still in force, and though this did not apply to the money brought in by the ferry, it did apply to dollars. It wasn't possible to credit dollars to an overseas account without permission from the Bank of England, nor could the banks issue foreign currency without a deal of red tape. Holidaymakers had to send in their passport and the amount they were taking out of the country was noted at the back. Beyond a certain fixed amount, permission would not be given.

So special arrangements had to be made to deal with the American servicemen based at Machrihanish, many of whom kept accounts at the branch. They would have a pay cheque made out in dollars and would ask for so much in dollars to spend at their own shops on the base, some in sterling for local shopping and the rest went into their account – in sterling. These were special 'nonresident accounts' and there was no difficulty about remitting the balance to America when a serviceman finished his tour of duty.

Iain had a very good understanding with the American Commander at that time. He was a country boy himself and was looking forward to the day when he could retire to the farm where he had grown up. He took a great interest in the local farms and his only complaint about this posting was the force of the winds at Machrihanish. He said it was the windiest base he'd ever served on. 'It doesn't matter which way the wind is blowing – it seems to blow straight through my house.' As the base is open to the Atlantic there is no shelter at all, and it didn't help to point out that the wind was probably coming straight from America.

Several British servicemen liked the place so much that they chose to settle in the town at the end of their service. Old Father Webb told Iain at their first meeting, 'People either can't stand the isolation and get away again within the first two years, or they stay for the rest of their lives. The Bishop said to me in 1931, "Give it eighteen months and see how you get on," – and I'm still here!' Father Webb was a local historian of note and he and his great friend, Duncan Colville, were both made Freemen of the Burgh in 1971 for the work they had done in researching and preserving the evidence of Campbeltown's fascinating history.

He was a great favourite in the bank, and latterly, when his eyesight had failed badly, he used to bring all his business papers into the office for Iain to read to him. It was a great pleasure to help him, but he always rewarded Iain with a bottle of sherry at Christmas. Latterly his eyesight got so bad that Iain was in the habit of making out his cheques for him and then all he had to do was to sign them. On one occasion, when Iain was out, Mr Grant performed this service for him, and, once he had collected his money, he immediately went over to Eaglesham's wine shop and bought a half-bottle of wine which he presented to Mr Grant. [Gordon was always referred to as Mr Grant, probably as a mark of respect because he was in a different age-bracket from the rest of the staff.]

After an embarrassed Gordon had thanked him and seen him safely out, he discovered that Father Webb had left his cheque-book behind, so he immediately phoned the old man's housekeeper and told her not to let him trail back for it as Iain would hand it in on his way home for lunch.

That afternoon the good Father returned and asked for Mr Grant.

'Have you still got that wine I gave you?' he demanded, and when Gordon indicated that he had, he continued, 'Well, I want it back!'

Mystified, because he couldn't think what he had done to give offence, Gordon handed it over and a few minutes later Father Webb arrived back with a full bottle! It was typical of the man, but his sight was so bad that the Campbeltown people did worry when they saw his frail figure out among the traffic in all weathers. Gordon had been trying to save him from an unnecessary and potentially dangerous visit, but it hadn't worked.

On another day, Iain had seen the old priest out and was going to escort him across the road when they met Mr MacTaggart, the organist at the Lowland Church.

'Good-morning, Mr MacTaggart,' Iain said, as this old man was another of his favourite customers.

'Good morning, Mr Rattray,' he replied in his lovely gentle Highland voice.

'I'm just going to see Father Webb here, across the street,' Iain explained.

'Oh, don't you worry, I'll look after Father Webb,' he said, and he took his arm. The two old men set off across the street and round the corner, chatting away like the old friends that they were. The point of this story is that Mr MacTaggart was totally blind, and had been since he was injured as a schoolboy.

'I've heard of the blind leading the blind,' Iain mused, 'but that's the first time I've seen it in action!'

Father Webb was a very old man, but nobody knew how old and it was his carefully cherished secret. Iain had to know to deal with official papers for him, but he was sworn to secrecy. When Father Webb eventually died, people thought that now, at last, they might find out. There was an enormous turn out at the funeral. All the churches were represented as he was universally loved, but a frisson of interest ran round the pews of the chapel when Father MacDonald began the eulogy.

'Father James Webb was born in Poulton, near Bristol, on 15th May...' * and there was a long pause. The congregation held its

---

* The date is fictional as I have not been able to verify the actual date given by the priest at the funeral.

breath and leant forward not to miss the all-important date. Father MacDonald smiled and completed the sentence, '...a very, very long time ago.' The mourners roared with laughter, they couldn't help themselves, and I'm sure that Father Webb, if he was looking down from heaven, laughed the longest!

Mr MacTaggart was a wonderful organist. He had taught music in one of the Glasgow colleges, in spite of his handicap, and though he was an old man when Iain knew him he was still playing regularly in the church. He was devoted to his wife and when she died Iain thought he might be broken. When he arrived at the church door to find the sons greeting the congregation as they arrived without their father, he was anxious for him and asked, 'Is your father not well?'

'He insisted on playing the organ for Mother,' he was told, and people who were there said he played as he had never played before.

Another lively old man among Iain's customers was the retired minister at Southend, the Rev Angus John MacVicar. Iain visited him at Southend and, by following the usual Highland custom of mutually exchanging family trees, Mr MacVicar worked out that the two families were related at some dim date in the past. Iain was never convinced of this, nor was Mr MacVicar's son, Angus, but it pleased the old man who must have been nearly ninety at the time, and it did no harm.

Angus, who was and is a well-known writer in Scotland, wrote a book in tribute to his father entitled, *Salt in my Porridge*. He had made a living from his pen all his life, though he had never written best-sellers. For some reason this book just took off and was followed by a series of autobiographical books which were very popular, especially with Scots overseas. Angus was delighted, and expressed his pleasure in one of the series entitled *Silver in my Sporran* where he says:

> *For forty-six years now I have been a customer at the Campbeltown branch of the Bank of Scotland. Managers like Albert Smith, Norval Charteris, Iain Rattray and Hamish McKinnon have all been friendly, in spite of the fact that frequently my current account has been overdrawn. Their help and advice – and practical encouragement in difficult times – has been invaluable to a temperamental author who can scarcely count up to ten, even on his fingers.*
>
> *Not so long ago I acquired a few shares in the Bank of Scotland and am intrigued to be called, after a hoary custom, a 'proprietor'. From impecunious reporter to 'proprietor' of a bank. 'Whaur's yer Andrew Carnegie noo?'*
>
> *Angus MacVicar,*
> *Silver in my sporran: confessions of a writing man*

It is true that shareholders in the Bank of Scotland are referred to as 'proprietors' and Iain always chuckles when he remembers, 'Angus was really chuffed about that!' Angus repaid any kindness he received from Iain many times over. He welcomed him into the drama group he ran in Southend and so opened the door to many friendships for us both, and he has given the most generous encouragement to my efforts to write.

The premises at 9 Longrow South had been the home of the old Union Bank before the amalgamation. The Bank of Scotland had been housed at 21 Longrow South and had used the same premises as the lawyers, Dick and MacKelvie, as a hundred years before, the original Mr Dick had been the lawyer-agent for the Bank of Scotland. Both businesses were combined at 9 Longrow South under Norval Charteris, the manager of the old Union Bank, and Mr Smith, the manager of the Bank of Scotland, was promoted to Helensburgh. The office at 9 Longrow was the bigger of the two offices but even so things were rather cramped and Iain's little box of an office was far from ideal. The bank owned the flat upstairs but when Iain suggested that it could be made use of Head Office refused, as they wanted all the staff under the eye of the accountant. The accountant was responsible for the running of the office. The manager was there to get in new business and keep the customers happy!

However, when the fishmonger's shop, next-door-but-one, fell empty, Iain saw his chance. First he went to see David Fairbairn of Stewart Balfour and Sutherland's who were acting for the seller, told him the bank might be interested, and asked him not to fix a closing date in the meantime. From there he went to see Bob Graham of Dick and MacKelvie's to ask if the owner of the sweet shop/tobacconist's next door would be willing to sell if the tenant was willing to move into the fish shop. He then had a word with Findlay Borthwick, the tenant, when he was buying his regular ten cigarettes and obtained his provisional agreement. Only then did he phone the Assistant Superintendent of Branches and put the whole complicated proposition in front of him. The senior man agreed to come down and have a look.

It was while Iain was doing his stint at the Highland Show that he was finally given permission to go ahead. Findlay was given help to convert the fish-shop but it took him a long time to get used to the fact that the shop was 'the wrong way round' as the new shop was the mirror image of the old one. None of the improvements to the office actually came about until after Iain had retired, but he took a lot of satisfaction from the fact that his friendly persuasion had actually worked!

The Bank of Scotland was one of the first banks to experiment with computerised accounting. Iain's first introduction to it took place when he was on a managers' course in Edinburgh and all the participants were taken to see the new machine in the office at 64 George Street. A whole room was devoted to the one computer – approaching it was rather like approaching a nuclear power station. Only a few bodies were allowed to enter the room at any one time in case their body heat raised the temperature of the room a degree or two and caused the thing to malfunction.

Iain said at the time, 'They took a lot more care of its well-being than they ever did of the human calculators in their employ. Imagine if we'd gone on strike whenever the temperature was a degree or two too hot or too cold for comfort!'

From time to time further bits of information filtered through and the advent of computerised banking became a regular topic at managers' training sessions. Iain is technophobic, and he was thankful that he was moving rapidly towards the end of his banking career, but the young couldn't wait to get their hands on the new technology. However, before that could come about there was a tremendous amount of rather boring preliminary work to be done. All the accounts had to be given numbers and all the standing orders had to be sorted and listed.

'I was only too happy to leave all that to Mr Grant,' he said, 'but I have a vivid memory of Jimmy MacNab and Kenneth MacConnachie on their knees on the customers' side of the counter after the doors had closed using the pattern of the tiles as a grid to sort out piles of standing orders.'

[I recalled Iain's comments about Mr Munro's detachment at the time of the amalgamation, and could see the parallel all too clearly but, at the time, I held my tongue. Discretion is almost always the better part of valour!]

A young man came down from Greenock every week and various machines were installed, but by this time Iain had opted out and was happy to concentrate on his own work and leave the rest to Mr Grant. Eventually the computer expert said, 'We'll be ready to transfer everything next Friday.'

Iain was taken aback, 'But I'm away on holiday next week,' he said. He was reassured.

'Don't you worry,' the young man said. 'Mr Grant and Jimmy and Kenneth have got it taped and they'll see to it. We'll be up and running when you come back.'

A week later he returned. 'Well Gordon, is that you on the computer now?'

Gordon looked sheepish. 'Well...no, I'm afraid not. It was to have been completed over the week-end, but there was a breakdown quite early on. We had barely started transferring the first ledger, and in the end Jimmy and Kenneth had to do it over our phone to a link in Kilmarnock and Jean and I had to get the use of Dick and MacKelvie's telephone to do the rest...and the young chap from Greenock is coming off the plane this morning.'

They were supposed to tap into the machines the account number and the balance for each current account. These figures should have been picked up in Ayr for onward transmission to Edinburgh, but as the link had broken down they had had to dictate the figures over the telephone – a long drawn out business. Then, to cap all, when the printouts came back from the computer on Tuesday, the totals didn't balance with the figures in the General Ledger. So they all had to be checked against the hand-posted ledger and the errors found and corrected in the time-honoured way. However, by the Wednesday the transfer was complete. Iain felt the staff deserved medals, but he was not exactly impressed by the new technology.

One of the difficulties was getting customers to remember their account numbers and to use them. People, especially those who remembered the war years, took a dim view of being reduced to a number. Once a week a print-out of all the customers' current account balances was sent to the branch, and, on one occasion, Iain noticed that a retired farm worker had a large increase in his credit balance. He asked Jean Cameron, 'Where did he get that money?' Jean didn't know and Iain suggested that she looked up the pay-in slip.

She returned a moment later and said, 'There's no pay-in slip – it's a repayment of VAT.'

Iain had just dealt with another customer who had complained that he would need an overdraft because, 'the Customs and Excise still haven't repaid my VAT.' Further investigation showed that two figures in his account number had been transposed. They made the necessary adjustments and all was well, but it didn't endear the system to Iain or to the individuals concerned. He reckoned that with the new technology it was even more important to know his customers.

When Mr MacKelvie, the retired senior partner of Dick and MacKelvie, visited the branch he was in the habit of dropping in to Iain's room for a chat, if Iain was free. Iain told him about the changes and asked him if he would like to see the computer working and, of course, he was curious so Iain took him through and asked Kenneth to demonstrate. Kenneth knew better than to ask Mr MacKelvie for his account number (he looked it up in the bank index) but then, with the air of a great magician, he turned to Mr MacKelvie and said, 'You see, Mr MacKelvie, I type in your account number and then the letters a-b-i-c and we wait!' He stepped back and a second later the machine began typing the details of Mr MacKelvie's account – without human assistance.

The old gentleman was horrified. He took a hasty step backwards and said, 'It isn't natural! It isn't natural!' – and immediately hurried out of the office shaking his head in dismay. Iain said, 'I'm sure he didn't believe what he had just seen – but Kenneth was so proud of his machine.' Never had the gulf between generations seemed so wide and so deep.

Iain felt, as his father had felt with the arrival of Burton's, that his skills had been overtaken. This was true in so far as mechanical accounting was concerned, but even now there is no substitute for the knowledge of human nature that is gained over a lifetime of caring about one's customers. The trend in recent years has been in the opposite direction. The banks compete with each other and with the lawyers and accountants with whom they used to co-operate, and the customer has not been the beneficiary. Iain saw the writing on the wall and was glad to get out, as were most of his contemporaries. He still gets a warm welcome in the office, as among his successors have been Hamish McKinnon, whom he had known as an apprentice in Lochgilphead, and John MacIntyre, who was the boy when he moved to Tarbert. Staff cuts have been much less savage in the Bank of Scotland than elsewhere, and the bank is good to its pensioners, but banking is not what it was and Iain is glad that he retired when he did.

We built a bungalow in Southend, using the services of a firm Iain had helped to get started, and the customers took a collection and bought him a superb greenhouse. We held a party for the staff and they presented him with a bag of golf clubs. Ian Bulloch came down, as did Archie MacNeill and his wife Marjorie. Barbara MacVicar was there, and spent the night with us in the new bungalow, and Kenneth, who had recently been posted, managed to get back to join the celebration.

A month later Iain joined A.I.B. Stewart of Stewart, Balfour and Sutherland, finding, at last, a use for his diploma in Executry!

Above: Iain's father outside the shop in George Street, Oban.

Left: Union Bank, Oban. July 1931

Interior, Union Bank, Oban. July 1931

Iain's father in the 'baby Austin' – bought 1926

Above: Jimmy Black driving the Austin with Jimmy's cousin Alastair Douglas and Iain in the back.

Left: 'Cewan' – Mrs MacEwan, Iain's landlady in Lochgilphead. 1937

Left: Iain in Mrs Westland's garden, Alva. 1938

Below: Bank house and Union Bank, Lochgilphead. Late 1930s

Left: NCC laying drains at Longtown (left to right – Len Smith, David Waddell, Iain, Bill Ward, Godfrey Dalton)

Right: With Ian Sim, son of the manager of Bank of Scotland, Lochgilphead. c1960

Left: The author – outside the conservatory I said would 'come down over my dead body!' Early 1970s

Right: Master of Ceremonies, 'Those were the Days', Tarbert Village Hall. c1965

Looking decidedly 'wolfish' with Jean Cameron, clerkess at the Campbeltown branch, outside the bank van at the Campbeltown Agricultural Show. Early 1970s

Iain's retirement party
(middle row – Archie MacNeill, Mary, Iain, Marjorie MacNeill, Ian Bulloch, Barbara MacVicar)